# Baptism

# Baptism

## A Biblical Study

# Jack Cottrell

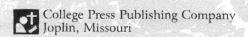
College Press Publishing Company
Joplin, Missouri

Toll-free order line 800-289-3300
On the web at www.collegepress.com
Unless otherwise noted, all scripture references are taken from the
NEW AMERICAN STANDARD BIBLE®, © Copyright 1960, 1962,
1963, 1968, 1971, 1972, 1973, 1975, 1977, 1995 by
The Lockman Foundation. Used by permission.
www.Lockman.org
Cover design by Brett Lyerla
**Library of Congress Cataloging-in-Publication Data**
Cottrell, Jack.
Baptism: a biblical study/ by Jack Cottrell.
p. cm.
Includes bibliographical references.
ISBN 0-89900-341-9 (softback)
1. Baptism—Biblical teaching. I. Title.
BS2655.B34C68 2006
234'.16109015—dc22                                              2006017598

# TABLE
# OF
# CONTENTS

# INTRODUCTION

The Bible is far from silent on the subject of baptism. Many clear and straightforward statements appear in both its narrative and its didactic sections. They are spread over the whole range of the New Testament, from the Gospels and Acts to the Pauline and General Epistles.

The main problem underlying the modern confusion on baptism thus is not paucity of Biblical material, but rather an *a priori* commitment to certain theological presuppositions. It is so extremely difficult — some would say impossible — to be objective when we try to interpret the Bible. We tend to read it, especially its references to baptism, with preconceived ideas of what it "must really be saying" or what it "surely cannot mean."

With full awareness of the difficulties involved, our goal in this study is to examine the main New Testament passages on the meaning of baptism as if we were hearing or seeing them for the first time. How would the original hearers of certain key statements have understood them? How would Nicodemus have understood John 3:5? How would Peter's audience have interpreted Acts 2:38? How did Paul understand Ananias' imperative in Acts 22:16? Also, how would the original readers of Acts and Romans and Colossians have interpreted the teaching on baptism contained therein? How would they have related this teaching to their own personal experience? For one who reads the New Testament today, what is the natural, face-value meaning of the passages on baptism? How would he under-

> Our goal in this study is to examine the main New Testament passages on the meaning of baptism.

stand the baptismal references if he had no prior knowledge of or commitment to any particular theological viewpoint, e.g., Reformed, Catholic, Lutheran, or "Campbellite"?

Though it is notoriously difficult to achieve, this should still be the goal of all exegesis or hermeneutics. We must reject all theories of hermeneutics that say the original meaning of a text is either irrecoverable or irrelevant. We must approach the Bible with the conviction that the original meaning of most texts, both as intended by their authors and as understood by their first recipients, is recoverable to a high degree of probability. Also, we must take this originally intended meaning as the definitive, authoritative one.

This is not to say that historical and theological perspectives have no place in the process of trying to achieve this goal. We must be ready to accept the help of anyone who has already studied the texts and has uncovered data relevant to their proper understanding. Also, we cannot ignore the valid limiting effect of systematic theology with reference to exegesis, especially if we believe in logical consistency. Unless we are irrationalists, we must believe that all Biblical doctrines are consistent with one another. Whatever is said about baptism must be consistent with whatever is said on other subjects such as sin, salvation, and the church. The relation between systematics and exegesis is somewhat dialectical. The data derived from the exegesis of the clearer texts must constantly be compared and collated, and the conclusions therefrom may legitimately be used in the exegesis of other (especially less clear) texts.

In spite of this dialectical relationship — or perhaps because of it — we must be very skeptical of any *system* that forces us to go against the natural and obvious meanings of any large number of texts especially on the same subject, such as baptism. We must question the validity of any system that requires us to interpret such texts in a consistently unnatural or strained manner or in a way that causes them to say something not actually found in the texts themselves. In other words, if the only reason for consistently doing violence to a whole category of texts is a dogmatic one, then we probably need to revise our theological system in a way that allows us to be true to the texts.

In any case our goal in this book is to let the texts speak as objectively as possible with a minimum of references to theological systems. Our main tools for understanding the texts will be linguistic, lexicographical, and background studies; and the time-honored hermeneutical rule of comparing Scripture with Scripture. Twelve key passages relevant to the meaning[1] of baptism will now be discussed in the order in which they appear in our English Bibles. (All Scripture quotations are from the New American Standard Bible except where noted.)

**NOTE**

1. It should be emphasized that the main focus of this study is the *meaning* of baptism, not its form and subjects. It is not my purpose to go into any detail on these latter aspects of baptism.

# ᴄ 1 ᴄ
# MATTHEW 28:19-20

The first New Testament reference to Christian baptism is in the Great Commission as recorded in Matthew 28:19-20. This implies of course that Christian baptism is distinct from all the Biblical baptisms which preceded it, including the baptism of Jesus by John, the baptism of John in general, and baptisms by Jesus' disciples. This distinction will be made clearer below. In any case the final instructions of Christ to his followers included these words: "Go therefore and make disciples of all the nations, baptizing them in the name of the Father and the Son and the Holy Spirit, teaching them to observe all that I commanded you" (Matt. 28:19-20).

The key term in this commission is "make disciples" in verse 19, translated "teach" in the King James Version. This is the only imperative among the verbs in these two verses; the other three elements of the commission are participles. "Going" is the prerequisite for making disciples; "baptizing" and "teaching" are the *means* of making disciples.

## Unique Importance

The first thing that strikes us about this passage is the fact that baptism is mentioned *at all* in such a terse and fundamental commission. It is also significant that it is distinguished from the category of "all things" which the disciples must be taught to observe. This is especially important in view of the common Protestant view that baptism is just one of the "good works" of

**11**

the Christian life, that it is just an "act of obedience" comparable to the many other acts of obedience that we are to perform simply because God has commanded them. If this is so, why is baptism alone singled out for specific mention, and why is it separated from "all that I commanded you"?

The way the commission is worded suggests that baptism has a unique importance in the process of disciple-making. We can agree that the term "all things" (Greek, *panta*) does refer to the

> The way the commission is worded suggests that baptism has a unique importance in the process of disciple-making.

good works or acts of obedience belonging to the Christian life; in other words it refers to the whole scope of sanctification that follows conversion. But the term is comprehensive (*"all* things"), and baptism is not included in it. The clear implication is that baptism is not meant to be placed in the category of Christian good works. It has a meaning distinct from any act of obedience expected of a Christian, and an importance far beyond that of any of these acts.

This unique importance of baptism is underscored by several other passages in the New Testament where baptism is mentioned but where it would be out of place if it were just another good work. One such passage is 1 Corinthians 1:10-17, which is often cited for just the opposite purpose, viz., to show the *un*importance of baptism. Here is what it says:

> Now I exhort you, brethren, by the name of our Lord Jesus Christ, that you all agree, and there be no divisions among you, but you be made complete in the same mind and in the same judgment. For I have been informed concerning you, my brethren, by Chloe's people, that there are quarrels among you. Now I mean this, that each one of you is saying, "I am of Paul," and "I of Apollos," and "I of Cephas," and "I of Christ." Has Christ been divided? Paul was not crucified for you, was he? Or were you baptized in the name of Paul? I thank God that I baptized none of you except Crispus and Gaius, that no man should say you were baptized in my name. Now I did baptize also the household of Stephanas; beyond that, I do not know whether I baptized any other. For Christ did not send me to

baptize, but to preach the gospel, not in cleverness of speech, that the cross of Christ should not be made void.

At first glance one might think that Paul is here demoting baptism to the ranks of insignificant duties or even optional acts. After all, he thanks God that he baptized only a few people (vv. 14,16), and says that his own commission was not to baptize but to preach the gospel (v. 17). But this is an incomplete and distorted reading of the passage for several reasons.

First, it ignores the *reason* why Paul is glad he baptized only a few, as verse 15 says, "that no man should say you were baptized in my name." Why is this important? Because in the early church baptism was so important that the human agent who did the baptizing often was made the object of special allegiance rivaling the worship of Christ and leading to factions within the church (see vv. 12-13). This danger was even more acute if the baptizer had an inherent prominence or authority, such as Peter, Paul, or Apollos. Paul is glad he baptized only a few so that the circle of his converts could not use this as a means of setting themselves apart from other Christians. His reasoning presupposes the *importance* of baptism, not its unimportance. Second, Paul's commission (v. 17) could not be materially different from that spoken by Christ in Matthew 28:19-20. Though Paul's own specific task was to preach the gospel, this was not to be *separated* from baptism. It simply means that he did not have to do the baptizing *personally*; he could leave that part of the commission to others, thus avoiding the potential for division. He obviously assumed that all his converts (and indeed all Christians) had been baptized, since he often referred to their baptism in his teaching (see Rom. 6:3ff; Gal. 3:27). Paul emphasizes the priority of his preaching since preaching *always* takes precedence over baptizing in the sense that it must always come first. Without preaching, there would not even be any faith (Rom. 10:14); and without faith, there would be no baptism in the first place.

Third, Paul's extensive teaching in other passages on the

**13**

important meaning of baptism (as discussed in chapters 7–12 below) would not be consistent with the view that he is denigrating baptism in this passage.

Finally, such a view contradicts the main lesson about baptism to be learned from 1 Corinthians 1:10-17, viz., that it is considered to be important enough to be listed in the most exclusive company. Verse 13 says, "Has Christ been divided? Paul was not crucified for you, was he? Or were you baptized in the name of Paul?" Here we see three things to be considered by those who are in danger of dividing the church through their secondary allegiances to human leaders: (a) The church is Christ's body. When you divide the church, you divide his very body. Do you want to be guilty of such an offense? (b) It was *Christ* who was crucified for you; it was Christ who performed the deed that purchased the church with his own blood. Don't put me (Paul) on this exalted level with Christ; I have not redeemed you. (c) You were baptized into the name of *Christ*, not Paul. Don't attach any human name to this act which relates you to the one head of the church.

The point is this: why should Paul bring up the subject of baptism at all, especially in conjunction with the momentous events of the crucifixion of Christ and the potential division of the body of Christ, if it were not among the most vital and serious aspects of the very existence and life of the church? How could he so forcefully and in the same breath remind them of who was crucified for them and of the name in which they were baptized, if baptism were not in some sense worthy of such a conjunction?

> Why should Paul bring up the subject of baptism at all if it were not among the most vital and serious aspects of the very existence and life of the church?

Another passage that takes baptism out of the category of Christian good works and reveals its unique importance is Ephesians 4:4-6, which lists the seven fundamental bases for Christian unity: "There is one body and one Spirit, just as also you were called in one hope of your calling; one Lord, one faith, one baptism, one God and Father of all who is over all and through all and in all." Again we are struck by the company baptism keeps! If baptism is relatively insignificant, or even if it has only equal significance with other Christian commands and duties, then of all such duties why should it be singled out and ranged here alongside items that occupy a much more lofty sphere of importance? Its companions are the three persons of the Trinity, the church (one body), heaven (one hope), and faith. Whether the "one faith" is objective (the one body of doctrine which is believed) or subjective (our common believing attitude) is a matter of disagreement. Even if it is the latter, then faith is the only other personal act (besides baptism) to be included in the list. How can we fail to see the significance of baptism's being included here, in some sense comparable in importance at least to faith itself? (See Hebrews 6:1-2 for a similar listing.)

Such passages as these help us to appreciate the wording of the commission in Matthew 28:19-20. They help us to understand why baptism is specifically mentioned and separated from the observing of all things commanded by Jesus. Baptism is not just obedience to another command, something typical of our Christian duty as a whole. Rather, it has a unique place in the commission and in the discipling process. Light is shed on the nature of this uniqueness in the record of one divinely directed instance of implementing the commission: Philip and the eunuch, Acts 8:26-40. In the context of evangelism, with a view to the eunuch's conversion, Philip "preached Jesus to him" (v. 35). This is the one-word summary of his preaching: *Jesus.* The only recorded response to this preaching is the eunuch's cry, "Look! Water! What prevents me from being baptized?" (v. 36). We cannot avoid the conclusion that the evangelistic preaching of Jesus includes the imperative of baptism. In terms of the Great Commission in Matthew 28:19-20, baptism is something taught *before* conversion with a view to *becoming* a disciple, while "teaching them to observe all that I commanded you" *follows* conversion and deals with the details of the Christian life.

**15**

# Into the Name

The element in the text itself that confirms the unique importance of baptism is the expression "in the name of the Father and the Son and the Holy Spirit" (v. 19). One is baptized literally *into the name* (Greek, *eis to onoma*) of the Trinity. What is the meaning of this expression, and what does it tell us about the meaning of baptism?

In the Biblical world a person's *name* was not just an arbitrary means of identification but was considered to be intrinsically related to the person himself, representing his qualities and his character and his very nature. Thus *"the name* of the Father and the Son and the Holy Spirit" (only one name) represents the very *persons* of the Trinity. Being baptized into the *name* of the Trinity is no less than being baptized into the Trinity as such.

What this means can be more precisely explained when we understand how the expression "into the name" was used in New Testament times. Many feel that Jesus probably spoke the Aramaic language; thus the phrase should be understood in its Semitic sense. The basic Semitic equivalent had a quite general meaning, viz., "with respect to or with regard to." In Rabbinic usage, though, it commonly had the more specific *final* sense. In this sense an action done "in the name" of something was done for a certain end or intention relating to it. Thus Jesus commissioned us to baptize people for a specific purpose relating to the Trinity, or into a specific relationship with the Trinity.[1]

The precise nature of this relationship can be learned from the usage of the Greek phrase chosen by Matthew (and approved by the Holy Spirit via inspiration) to translate whatever Semitic original may have preceded it. The phrase is *"eis to onoma"* which was a technical term used in the world of Greek business and commerce. It was used to indicate the entry of a sum of money or an item of property into the account bearing the name of its owner.[2] Its use in Matthew 28:19 indicates that the purpose of baptism is to unite us with the Triune God in an *ownership* relation; we become his property in a special, intimate way.[3] As M.J. Harris says, since the phrase denotes transference of ownership, in Matthew 28:19 it means that "the person being baptized passes into the possession of the Triune God."[4]

> The purpose of baptism is to unite us with the Triune God in an ownership relation; we become his property in a special, intimate way.

From this specific meaning of the phrase we can see why we are baptized "into the name of" the entire Trinity. God the Father paid the price to acquire us as his property, namely, the blood of God the Son (1 Cor. 6:19-20; 1 Pet. 1:18-19). He also applies the seal which marks us as his own, namely, God the Holy Spirit (Eph. 1:13). All of this comes into sharp focus in baptism, where the purchase price — Christ's blood — is applied to us (Rom. 6:3-4; Col. 2:12) and the mark of ownership — the Holy Spirit — is given to us (Acts 2:38). Thus we are baptized "into the name of the Father and of the Son and of the Holy Spirit"; we become God's own special possession in the act of baptism. No wonder it is singled out in the commission as having a unique importance!

## A New Condition

The discussion of Matthew 28:19-20 has suggested that baptism is not to be equated with ordinary acts of obedience but is rather to be regarded as a conversion experience that brings us into a union with God Himself. Thus what is known even from this one passage warrants the assessment that baptism has a *saving* significance — a conclusion that will be even more inescapable in view of the other passages to be discussed below. In fact, it would appear that God is instituting baptism as a *new condition* for salvation in the New Testament era, in addition to what was required in pre-Christian times (viz., faith and repentance). Why should this be so? The answer may be found in Matthew 28:19-20 as we reflect on the fact that Christian baptism is baptism into the name of the *Trinity*.

Some may find it difficult to accept the idea that God would add a condition for salvation in the Messianic age, thereby apparently making it more difficult to be saved today than in the Old Testament period. If faith and repentance were able to secure a right relationship with God then, why should it be any different now? The answer lies in the very fact that we have passed into a new age, an age marked especially by the actual accomplishment of the works of redemption and a fuller revelation of the Trinitarian nature of God in connection with these works. This transition is so radical that not only is a new condition added, but even the old conditions have been changed.

Sufficient attention has not been given to the fact that the *faith* required for salvation in this age is not the same as the faith that sufficed in the earlier age. In that era anyone who surrendered to the exclusive Lordship of the God of Israel and trusted His gracious promise of mercy was accepted by God. This included all the Jews who put their heart-felt trust in the One God who revealed Himself in their midst, as well as any Gentiles who knew this revelation of the true God and followed Him from their hearts. Examples of the latter would be the Ninevites in Jonah's time (Jonah 3:10) and Cornelius even before he knew Christ (Acts 10:1-2).

> Sufficient attention has not been given to the fact that the faith required for salvation in this age is not the same as the faith that sufficed in the earlier age.

It is quite sobering, however, to realize that the faith that sufficed for salvation and marked one as devout in that age was no longer sufficient once that person had come to know the fuller revelation of the New Testament gospel. Once the facts of the gospel were known, even the most devout Old Testament believer was faced with this choice: either accept the fuller revelation of the God of Israel, or be transferred to the ranks of unbelievers. A person could be saved one moment by his faith in the God he knew from the Old Covenant revelation, and be lost the next moment for refusing to accept Jesus as the redeeming presence and fuller revelation of this same God. Surely the thousands who were gathered in Jerusalem at the time of Pentecost (Acts 2) included some of the most devout Jews, the spiritual "cream of the crop," so to speak. But once they had heard the gospel, they were counted as sinners unless and until they accepted Jesus as their Savior. This would have been true of any Jewish audience being evangelized in this rather awkward period of transition from Old Testament faith to New Testament faith, including Saul (who heard Stephen's sermon. Acts 7:57–8:1) and the eunuch (who was evangelized by Philip, Acts 8:26ff). This point is clear from Paul's analogy of the olive tree in Romans 11:16ff, where he says the previously-believing Jews (natural branches of the tree) were broken off the tree because of their unbelief (v. 20) but may be grafted into the tree again if they do not continue in their unbelief (v. 23).

Two things account for this radical change in the nature of saving faith. First, the actual works of redemption are now accomplished facts, and saving faith must be directed toward them specifically and not just toward the general promises of a merciful God. We now know that forgiveness of sins is possible only because of the blood of Christ shed on the cross; thus faith must now be "faith in his blood" (Rom. 3:25, NIV). We now know that eternal life is possible only because of the resurrection of Jesus from the dead; thus you must now "believe in your heart that God raised Him from the dead" (Rom. 10:9). We now know that since Pentecost the Holy Spirit has been poured out from heaven and is offered to us as a regenerating and sanctifying presence; thus our faith must now embrace this specific promise of the Spirit (Acts 2:38-39).

The second thing that requires a change in the nature of saving faith is the fact that these works of redemption have been accomplished by a God who is *Triune* in nature. Though the concept of the Trinity was foreshadowed in the Old Testament revelation, its reality was never made explicit. But when the time came for God's redemptive work actually to be accomplished in history, the triunity of God's being could no longer be concealed, since the distinct acts of redemption were wrought by distinct persons within the Trinity. Thus any saving faith in God today must be in the God who has actually saved us, namely, the God who is Father, Son, and Holy Spirit. A denial of the Trinity is no less than

**19**

a denial of the very Saviorhood of God. These two things — faith in the One God who is Three Persons, and faith in the saving works of God — are now inseparably linked.

Herein lies the reason for the addition of baptism as a new condition for salvation in this age. The change in the content of saving faith made it expedient to add this most appropriate condition, not as a new condition per se, but as a concrete embodiment of this radically different faith itself. It makes abundantly clear the fact that an Old Testament type of faith in God is no longer adequate, and that one must commit himself to faith in the Triune God for salvation. Herein also lies the reason why baptism is specifically a baptism into the name of the Father and of the Son and of the Holy Spirit. In this act the exclusive role of God the Son in our redemption is indelibly impressed upon our minds, as in baptism we are buried into his death and resurrection for the remission of our sins (Rom. 6:3-5; Acts 2:38). In this act the presence of God the Spirit becomes a reality in our lives, as baptism is the time God has chosen to give us "the gift of the Holy Spirit" (Acts 2:38). It is God's way of requiring us to lift our faith up to the level of the New Testament revelation of the trinitarian dimension of God's own nature and of the work of salvation itself.

This is why no pre-Pentecostal baptism can be equated with Christian baptism. The baptism of John was given and practiced in the age of Old Testament faith, before the trinitarian redemption had actually been accomplished and before a trinitarian relationship with God was even possible. It was indeed a "baptism of repentance for the forgiveness of sins" (Luke 3:3), but the specific relationship with the cross and the blood of Christ could not yet be explained. Also, the gift of the Holy Spirit was not yet available (John 7:37-39). Thus it is a serious error to think that John's baptism and Christian baptism are the same in their meaning and significance. On the day of Pentecost no exceptions were allowed for those who may have received John's baptism: "Repent and be baptized, *every one of*

> It is a serious error to think that John's baptism and Christian baptism are the same in their meaning and significance.

*you*" (Acts 2:38, NIV). Paul gave Christian baptism to those who had received only John's baptism, specifically because the latter lacked the trinitarian content (Acts 19:1-6). Few serious lessons can be learned about Christian baptism from the practice of John's baptism, including his baptism of Jesus. It is quite inappropriate to use Jesus' baptism as a model or example for baptism today, either in its necessity or its meaning.

The relation between baptism and the Trinity is thus of extreme importance, and the significance this act receives from its inseparable connection with trinitarian faith is difficult to exaggerate. When we give to baptism a significance anything less than that described in the New Testament and in Matthew 28:19-20 in particular, we are weakening the significance of the profound historical transition from the Old Testament pretrinitarian faith in God to the New Testament trinitarian faith, a transition that Jesus Christ himself has tied to Christian baptism. Also, when we fail to use the trinitarian formula in the baptismal service itself, we are ignoring one of the principal elements of the newness of this new age. Such neglect does not necessarily invalidate a baptism, but it surely shows little respect for Jesus' commission, and it wastes a prime opportunity to testify to our trinitarian faith and to impress upon the convert the fact that he owes his salvation to the work of the Father and the Son and the Spirit.[5]

## Summary

Concerning the meaning of baptism as reflected in Matthew 28:19-20 we have made the following points. First, the very fact that baptism is specifically mentioned in the commission and also the fact that it is distinguished from acts of ordinary obedience indicate that it has a unique importance in the process of disciple-making. Second, the essence of this importance is that baptism is "into the name" of the Triune God; in it we become God's own possession. Finally, the New Covenant necessity for a specifically trinitarian faith is the rationale for adding baptism as a new condition for salvation, since by design it relates us to the Trinity both in symbol and in fact.

## NOTES

1. Hans Bietenhard, "ὄνομα, etc.," *Theological Dictionary of the New Testament,* ed. Gerhard Friedrich, tr. Geoffrey W. Bromiley (Grand Rapids: Eerdmans, 1967), V:274-275.

2. Albrecht Oepke, "βάπτω, etc.," *Theological Dictionary of the New Testament,* ed. Gerhard Kittel, tr. Geoffrey W. Bromiley (Grand Rapids: Eerdmans, 1964), 1:539.

3. See G. R. Beasley-Murray, *Baptism in the New Testament* (Grand Rapids: Eerdmans, 1962), 90-91.

4. Murray J. Harris, "Appendix: Prepositions and Theology in the Greek New Testament," *The New International Dictionary of New Testament Theology,* ed. Colin Brown (Grand Rapids: Zondervan, 1978), 111:1209.

5. Some of this material has already appeared in the author's book, *What the Bible Says About God the Redeemer* (Joplin, Mo.: College Press, 1987), 171-173.

**The following baptisms are without Scriptural foundation and often lead to confusion when people are shown the New Testament example.** *Luke 7:30*

1. A baptism without *Faith* .

   **Acts 18:8b** *"and many of the Corinthians who heard him believed and were baptized."*

   *Mark 16:16*
   *Acts 8:36,37*

2. A baptism without *Repentance* .

   **Acts 2:38** *"Peter replied, repent and be baptized, every one of you, in the name of Jesus Christ for the forgiveness of your sins and you will receive the gift of the Holy Spirit."*

   *Math 3:7-8*        *4 Examples*
                       *W/o Rep*     *1- Peer*
                                     *2- Friends Dare*
                                     *3- Satisfy parents*
                                     *4- Children*
                                     *Proons (Parents)*

3. A baptism without the *forgiveness* of *sins* .

   **Acts 22:16** *"And now what are you waiting for? Get up, be baptized and wash away your sins calling on the name of the Lord."*

   *Acts 9:1*              *Jeremiah 4:14*
   *1 Peter 3:21*
   *Holdid Zwingly*

4. A baptism without the gift of the *Holy Spirit* .

   **Acts 19:2b** *"Did you receive the Holy Spirit when you believed? They answered, "No, we have not even heard that there is a Holy Spirit."* **Acts 19:5** *"On hearing this, they were baptized into the name of the Lord Jesus."*

   *Acts 5:32*

# "Baptismal Confusion"
## Acts 19:1-5

There is no subject in the Bible about which there is more misunderstanding than the subject of baptism; it is a watershed issue. There is a difference of understanding in Christendom of the mode/practice of baptism, the candidate to be baptized, and the purpose of baptism. This is sad because the subject of baptism by itself divides people of faith, and Jesus prayed for the unity of His followers (John 17:20-21). We shouldn't be surprised by this division because the devil is a master at questioning and altering what God's word says (Gen. 3:1-6).

Where did all this confusion arise humanly speaking? One primary answer is the Swiss reformer, Huldreich Zwingli. For the first 1500 years of the church, baptism was considered a salvation event. Zwingli said everyone before him was wrong about their understanding of baptism. He taught that baptism was the New Testament replacement for Old Testament circumcision. Circumcision was the sign that a child belonged to a Jewish family. Zwingli said baptism is a sign that the parents are going to raise their child in a Christian home, but he denied that baptism was a salvation event.

The following ideas are just a few of the *incorrect* assumptions that people have about the subject of baptism.

- **Baptism is a work of law that contradicts salvation by grace**. Salvation is a gift of God (Rom. 6:23), but baptism is not a work of law, but is a response to the gospel. *Where does the New Testament categorize baptism as a work of law?*

- **Baptism is for church membership**. Baptism makes a person a member of the body of Christ/church (1 Cor. 12:13) when they are saved, but many people practice baptism to join a church. *Where does the New Testament say you baptize for church membership?*

- **Baptism is an outward sign of an inward grace.** This popular idea teaches that forgiveness happens when you pray for forgiveness, and baptism is the outward sign of an inward forgiveness already received. *Where does the New Testament say that baptism is an outward sign of an inward grace?*

- **Baptism is water washing away sins.** Water removes dirt, but not sins; only the blood of Jesus can handle such "stains!" Did the fruit Adam and Eve ate take away their innocence? No, the fruit was neutral—disobedience took away their innocence. The water of baptism is just water, but in the obedience of baptism God forgives sins.

# ⚊2⚊
# MARK 16:15-16

The next New Testament reference to Christian baptism is in Mark's summary of the Great Commission: "And He said to them, 'Go into all the world and preach the gospel to all creation. He who has believed and has been baptized shall be saved; but he who has disbelieved shall be condemned" (Mark 16:15-16). Since this passage appears in a disputed section of the Greek text, one could argue that it should not be discussed here at all. The last twelve verses of Mark (16:9-20) appear in the *Textus Receptus* version of the Greek testament (which underlies the King James Version), but more recent manuscript evidence has led most scholars to conclude that this was a later addition to Mark's Gospel and thus should not be considered a part of the inspired canon. The editors of the United Bible Societies Greek text find it "virtually certain" that verses 9-20 should be omitted.

Without trying to resolve the textual issue, we shall proceed on the working assumption that Mark 16:16 is canonical. Even if this should prove not to be the case (which actually appears to be the more probable conclusion), the Biblical doctrine of baptism would not be diminished thereby. Nothing is learned from this verse that cannot be learned from other New Testament teaching about baptism.

## Baptism and Faith

It is universally accepted that faith is and always has been an essential condition for salvation. See John 3:16; Acts 16:31;

**23**

Ephesians 2:8. What strikes us first about Mark 16:16 is that faith and baptism are linked together so intimately in this context. If anything at all were going to be put into such a relationship with faith, there are other things that might at first seem more appropriate than baptism. For example, we would not have been surprised at "He who has believed and has called on the name of the Lord shall be saved" (Acts 2:21). Or, "He who has believed and has repented shall be saved" (Mark 1:15; Acts 20:21). Or, "He who has believed and has confessed Christ shall be saved" (Rom. 10:9-10). Actions such as prayer, repentance, and confession would appear to have a kind of family resemblance to faith, whereas baptism seems to be a different kind of act altogether.

This is why it is so important to note the close conjunction of faith and baptism in this commission. It should cause us to re-examine our preconceptions about baptism and to realize that it is not so different from faith after all. This is borne out by other passages that bring the two together. We have

> In the New Testament all the gifts of grace promised to faith are also promised to baptism.

already commented on Ephesians 4:5 in the preceding chapter. Two others that should be carefully noted are Galatians 3:26-27 and Colossians 2:12. Beasley-Murray notes and documents the fact that in the New Testament all the gifts of grace promised to faith are also promised to baptism.[1]

What is the focus of the faith enjoined upon us in Mark 16:16? Like all saving faith, it must be directed toward God's promises of mercy and salvation. In this age it must be directed specifically toward Jesus Christ and His saving work of atonement and resurrection. This is one reason why faith has a natural affinity with baptism, viz., because baptism in its very action symbolizes the death, burial, and resurrection of Christ (see Romans 6:3ff). God's word of promise, which we believe, is visualized in Christian baptism, so that baptism itself becomes a kind of visualization of faith.

But there is more. Baptism not only embodies the primary objects of our faith and the promises connected therewith, but also *is itself* a promise (see the section "Baptism as Promise"

**24**

This is the most reasonable explanation for the omission of baptism in the second clause, which would most likely be understood in this way by anyone seeing the statement for the first time and without theological bias. A second possible explanation has been suggested, however, distinguishing between what is *absolutely* necessary for salvation as compared with what is only *relatively* necessary. The idea is that even if baptism has been appointed by God as a necessary part of the salvation process in the New Testament age, it still has only a relative necessity and can be dispensed with in extraordinary circumstances. The only absolutely and inherently necessary condition for salvation is faith; thus it alone is mentioned in the second clause. It is conceivable that one could be saved without baptism, but not without faith.

This distinction has been recognized all through Christian history. The "baptism of blood" and the "baptism of desire" have been accepted as valid substitutes for baptism in water in circumstances where water baptism is physically impossible. "Baptism of blood" refers to martyrdom; it refers to situations in which a person has put his faith in Christ but is martyred for his faith before he has a chance to be baptized. (This possibility was quite prevalent in the early Christian centuries when initial faith and baptism were often separated by lengthy periods of catechetical instruction.) "Baptism of desire" refers to *any* situation in which a believer honestly desires to meet the condition of baptism but is prevented from doing so by irremedial physical circumstances, e.g., confined to prison, nailed to a cross, pinned down by enemy gunfire, lost in a desert. In such cases it is reasonable to assume that God "takes the will for the deed" and saves a person without baptism, as long as he believes on the Lord Jesus Christ.

In this connection we must be careful to guard against an error that is quite common within Protestantism, namely, a glossing over of the distinction between absolute and relative necessity as it refers to baptism. It is common practice to cite a situation in which water baptism for a believer is impossible (e.g., lost in a desert) and to conclude from such that baptism has *no* necessary connection with

**27**

> In any normal situation where water baptism is at all possible, it is a condition for salvation.

salvation at all. That is to say, an example that proves at most that baptism is not *absolutely* necessary is used to prove that it is not necessary even under *ordinary* circumstances. This is a *non sequitur*: it does not follow. In any normal situation where water baptism is at all possible, it is a condition for salvation: "He who has believed and has been baptized shall be saved."

"The thief on the cross" is commonly misused in this context. In the first place, how the believing thief was saved is irrelevant for the Christian era since he was still under the old covenant and since Christian baptism did not even exist yet. In the second place, even if his case were relevant, it would be an example only of the "baptism of desire" (not blood or martyrdom) and would prove only that baptism does not share the *absolute* necessity of faith. It says nothing about what might be required under ordinary circumstances; it cannot be used to negate the clear and simple affirmation in the first clause of Mark 16:16.

# Baptism as Promise

Many will have difficulty accepting so close a relation between baptism, faith, and salvation as it is taught in Mark 16:16. This is because of the widespread acceptance of the idea discussed earlier, that baptism is just one of many commands addressed to Christians, obedience to which constitutes "good works." What must be understood is that the basic essence of baptism is more that of a *promise* than a command.

Commands are basically the imperatives of the Creator and Lawgiver to his creatures *as creatures*. They tell us what we should do in order to be true to our own nature and in order to honor God: "You do this." On the other hand, promises are basically the word of God the Redeemer to his creatures *as sinners*. They tell us what God has done and will do in order to save us: "I have done this; I will do this."

Baptism falls more into the latter category than the former. In the imperative of baptism, God is not so much commanding us to do something as He is promising to do something for us. Whoever believes and is baptized shall be saved: this is a promise. Whoever repents and is baptized for the remission of sins shall receive the gift of the Holy Spirit: this is a promise (Acts 2:38-39). Is this not what the sinner needs? He does not need more commandments or laws; he needs the promise of help, the promise of forgiveness, the promise of a way out, a way of escape from the predicament of sin. This is exactly what baptism is. It is God's promise to meet us in that moment and give us forgiveness and new life.

This is how the person being baptized should be instructed to think of his imminent baptism. He is not just obeying an imperative but is also accepting a promise from the gracious God, the promise of something he desperately needs. Here in Mark 16:16 the very form of the statement is that of a promise. It is true that sometimes the instruction concerning baptism is in the grammatical form of a command, as in Acts 2:38 and Acts 22:16. But in essence these imperatives do not have the character of a "boss's orders." They are more comparable to a doctor's instruction to someone who is very ill: "Do you want to get well? Then take this medicine." Though the instruction is in the grammatical form of an imperative, a sick person would not respond to it as if he were obeying a command. He would accept it as a word of promise and hope; he would comply with eager expectation of receiving the benefits of the doctor's knowledge and work. Imperatives concerning baptism may also be compared to the words of a rescuer who throws a line to a drowning man: "Grab this rope!" The rope would immediately and gratefully be seized as a promise of salvation. Likewise when the sinner hears the words "Be baptized," he should respond as if accepting the promise of salvation: "He who has believed and has been baptized shall be saved."

This applies not only to the sinner who is about to be baptized, but also to Christians whose baptism is an event of the past. This

**29**

| | |
|---|---|
| **God promised to cover our sins with the blood of His dear Son.** | is especially meaningful when we begin to be discouraged about our Christian growth or are tempted to doubt our salvation. We can look back to that concrete and objective reference point in our experience where |

God promised to cover our sins with the blood of His dear Son and to accept us from that moment on just as if we had never sinned. Thus the promise of baptism is a source of continuing strength and encouragement throughout our Christian lives.

## Summary

What do we learn from Mark 16:15-16 about the meaning of baptism? First, the fact that it is intimately conjoined with believing suggests that it has more of the character of faith than that of works. Second, God has appointed baptism as a condition for salvation in any normal situation where it can be performed. Third, though baptism is an imperative that must be obeyed, the essence of baptism is more akin to a promise than a command.

### NOTE

1. Beasley-Murray, *Baptism in the Ne\v Testament,* 272-273.

# ~3~
# JOHN 3:3-5

The third New Testament passage reflecting on the meaning of baptism is John 3:3-5, which is part of Jesus' conversation with Nicodemus about the necessity of the new birth:

> Jesus answered and said to him, "Truly, truly, I say to you, unless one is born again, he cannot see the kingdom of God." Nicodemus said to Him, "How can a man be born when he is old? He cannot enter a second time into his mother's womb and be born, can he?" Jesus answered, "Truly, truly, I say to you, unless one is born of water and the Spirit, he cannot enter into the kingdom of God."

Though not everyone agrees that the word *water* in verse 5 refers to baptism, such a strong case can be made for it that this has been the predominant view throughout Christian history.

## Water and Baptism

If the water in John 3:5 does not refer to baptism, then to what *does* it refer? Two main alternatives have been suggested. First, some try to equate the water-birth of verse 5 with *physical* birth, the water itself referring to amniotic fluid. Though verse 4 does introduce the idea of physical birth into the context, the term for water is never used in this sense elsewhere in the New Testament. Verse 6 uses a different term to characterize physical birth, namely, "born of flesh." This is the common expression for ordinary physical birth when contrasted with spiritual or supernatural birth (John 1:13; Rom. 1:3; Gal. 4:23,29). Another problem is that this interpretation would have Christ saying, "Unless a person is born physically, he cannot be saved" — an awkward and puzzling affirmation to say the least.

The second main alternative is that *"water* here is used figuratively as a symbol of the Holy Spirit. Such a figure may be found elsewhere in Scripture, as in Isaiah 44:3 and John 7:37-39. It is most likely also that Jesus' reference to "living water" in John 4:10-14 points to the Holy Spirit, though the latter is not specifically mentioned in the context. Thus such a usage in John 3:5 would not be conceptually alien either to the Bible as a whole or to John's Gospel in particular. Counting against this view is the straightforward, prosaic nature of Jesus' statement in John 3:5, and the lack of any contextual indication of a figurative intention for the term. For example, here he uses only the bare and unqualified term *water*, whereas in both John 4:10-14 and John 7:37-39 he speaks of the Spirit as *living water*. Also, in these latter two passages, there is a contextual contrast between ordinary water and living water offered by Jesus. Such a contrast is absent in John 3:5. Finally, in John 3:5, the expression "born of water and the Spirit" is so terse and tight that there is really no room for symbolic maneuvering (as there is in the poetic parallelism of Isaiah 44:3, for example). There are simply two nouns, both of which are objects of the one preposition "of" *(ek)* and are joined by the simple conjunction "and" *(kai)*. Some have sought to identify water and Spirit here by translating *kai* as "even," viz., "born of water, even the Spirit." But the terseness of the expression plus the other considerations listed above would permit this interpretation only if there were no other reasonable and readily recognizable referent for the word *water*. But such is not the case. In both the historical and literary contexts the term *water* would immediately call to mind the common practice of baptism in water.

When Nicodemus heard Jesus' words for the first time, he had several good reasons to apply them to baptism. We who read them today in the light of other New Testament teaching have these and even more such reasons. First of all, the fame of the ministry of John the Baptist, highlighted by the novelty of his baptizing repentant Jews (rather than allowing them to baptize themselves, as in Essene and proselyte baptisms), cannot be

When Nicodemus heard Jesus' words for the first time, he had several good reasons to apply them to baptism.

overemphasized. All Israel knew that John baptized in water (see John 1:26-31). Nicodemus could not have helped but connect Jesus' words with John's work.

Second, Jesus' own baptism by John, which must have been widely reported in that day and which is recorded for our reading, involved a conjunction of water baptism and the descent of the Spirit. See Matthew 3:16; Mark 1:10; Luke 3:21-22; John 1:32-33. Thus a reference to "water and Spirit" would not unnaturally cause us to think of baptism.

Third, John the Baptist's teaching contained a strong emphasis on the distinction between water baptism and Spirit baptism. See Matthew 3:11; Luke 3:16; John 1:33. This is capsulized in Mark 1:8, "I baptized you with water; but He will baptize you with the Holy Spirit." Thus again, when "water and Spirit" are mentioned together in John 3:5, we would quite naturally think of baptism.

Fourth, another aspect of John's teaching was the relation between his water baptism and the coming kingdom (Matt. 3:2). Thus in John 3:5, when Jesus relates water and the kingdom, it again brings baptism to mind.

The four items above would apply to anyone who knew of John the Baptist's ministry, including Nicodemus. The fifth and last reason for understanding Jesus' reference to water to mean baptism would apply only to those who know the teaching of the whole New Testament. I am referring to the interrelation of the concepts of baptism, birth, and resurrection. This passage refers to being "born of water." Do any other New Testament passages specifically speak of baptism as a birth? No, but two important texts speak of it as a resurrection from spiritual death, namely, Romans 6:4-5 and Colossians 2:12. This is significant because in Scripture resurrection and birth are figuratively intertwined. Colossians 1:18 and Revelation 1:5 speak of Jesus as the "first-born

> **"Raised up in baptism" and "born of water" are equivalent concepts.**

from the dead" (see Romans 8:29). Acts 13:33 equates the raising up of Jesus with the day of his begetting. Thus "raised up in baptism" and "born of water" are equivalent concepts, and we are justified in taking John 3:5 as a reference to baptism.

Some who agree that this refers to baptism think that John's baptism or even Jewish proselyte baptism must be in view, since these are the only kinds of baptism with which Nicodemus would have been familiar. We need not limit the specific reference to something in his experience, however. Jesus taught publicly about other future events and future blessings without explaining them as such. He spoke thus of his victorious resurrection: "Destroy this temple, and in three days I will raise it up" (John 2:19-22). His statement concerning the living water in John 7:37-39 referred to the Pentecostal outpouring of the Spirit. Some think His teaching about eating His flesh and drinking His blood (John 6:53ff) has to do with the Lord's Supper. Thus Christian baptism cannot be excluded from John 3:5 simply because it had not been instituted yet. In fact, even the second part of the statement, "born of Spirit," is itself a reference to the future Christian era, since regeneration via the indwelling Holy Spirit was a blessing offered only after Pentecost (John 7:37-39; Acts 2:38-39).

Some complain that those who are more inclined to a sacramentalist view of baptism are guilty of indiscriminately interpreting every Biblical reference to water as a reference to baptism.[1] In the early Christian centuries such a complaint would have been justified in view of the excessively allegorical hermeneutic of the church fathers, but such is hardly the case today. Of the nearly 80 occurrences of the Greek word for water *(hudor)* in the New Testament, there are only three disputed passages where anything is at stake: John 3:5; Ephesians 5:26; and Hebrews 10:22. Of the other references, about 30 speak of ordinary water in non-baptismal situations. Eighteen other uses occur in the book of Revelation, where scenes of apocalyptic symbolism include a variety of fountains and streams. Five times John mentions "water and blood" in connection with Jesus' ministry and death. There are 16 undisputed references to water baptism (both John's and Christian),[2] and seven undisputed figurative uses.[3] In view of the fact that *water* indisputably means baptism in twenty percent of its occurrences, it is surely not unreasonable to interpret it this way in the three disputed passages if such is exegetically and theologically warranted. This is especially true in view of the fact that *water* is indisputably used in a figurative sense less than ten percent of the time, and this on only two occasions (John 4:10-15 [6 times] and John 7:38 [once]). In view of the comparative distribution of the term, there is more justification for seeing water baptism in the three disputed passages, including John 3:5, than for excluding it therefrom.

## Entering the Kingdom

This passage is without question dealing with salvation and with an essential condition thereof in the Christian age. The salvation is called "seeing (or entering) the kingdom of God"; the condition is "being born again."

The basic meaning of the Biblical words for *kingdom* is kingship or reign or dominion; the "kingdom of God" is the reign of God. A secondary meaning is the realm over which the king reigns. A major theme of Old Testament prophecy is the coming of the kingdom. A typical statement is Daniel 2:44, "And in the days of those kings the God of heaven will set up a kingdom which will never be destroyed." This was the major element in the eschatological hope of the Jews; they were "waiting for the kingdom of God" (Mark 15:43). John the Baptist's message was so electrifying because he was declaring the imminence of this kingdom: "Repent, for the kingdom of heaven is *at hand*" (Matt. 3:2). This was Jesus' message, too (Matt. 4:17).

In one sense the coming of Jesus Himself *was* the coming of the kingdom, since God the King was present as Jesus Christ for the very purpose of establishing His Lordship over all of creation.

The events which decisively accomplished this purpose were His death, resurrection, and ascension to glory. This was the establishment of His kingdom in the sense of His *reign*. The kingdom in the sense of the *realm* over which He reigns is made up of those who willingly acknowledge and surrender to Christ's Lordship, viz., those who make the "good confession" that Jesus is Lord. In its identifiable concrete form, the kingdom-realm is the church. The two are apparently equated in Matthew 16:18-19.

Thus from the perspective of Nicodemus, the kingdom was still a future reality; but like all good Jews he would be anxiously awaiting it and eager to enter it and be a part of it. Jesus is here telling him (and all of us) what would be necessary for entrance into the kingdom once it was established. (There is no significant difference between *seeing* the kingdom [verse 3] and *entering* it [verse 5].)

"Entering the kingdom" is a soteriological idea. To a Jew like Nicodemus, It would be the ultimate salvation experience. To non-Jewish people today or to anyone not steeped in the eschatological hope of the Old Testament, the expression does not immediately conjure up all the connotations of salvation; but that is its intent. To enter the kingdom is to surrender to the Lordship of Christ and thus to enter the state of grace and the realm of salvation.

> To enter the kingdom is to surrender to the Lordship of Christ.

## Born Again

Jesus' basic affirmation in John 3:3-5 is that being *born again* is an essential condition for entering the kingdom. In verse three He uses the word *anothen*, which can mean either "from above" or "again." The dominant idea here seems to be the latter. At least Nicodemus seemed to have understood it this way. In his response (verse 4) he asks whether it is possible for an old man "a second time" to enter his mother's womb and be born. Though the word itself points to the idea of rebirth, Jesus' reply (verse 5) indicates that the second birth is indeed a birth "from above" insofar as it is accomplished by the Spirit. The concept of being "born of God" is prevalent in John's writings.[4] It is a supernatural act which only God, in the person of the Holy Spirit, can perform.

The concept of "born again" is identical to the concept of personal regeneration as it occurs in Titus 3:5. The Greek expressions are practically equivalent in meaning. This new birth or regeneration is the change that takes place in the sinner's inner nature during his conversion. It is one of the two main aspects of the "double cure" that God offers to the sin-sick. The first aspect is justification or forgiveness, which changes our objective relationship to God and His law by removing the guilt and penalty of our sins. This second aspect addresses the fact that sin has corrupted our hearts and souls with an inner depravity; it has infected our spirits with weakness and sickness and even spiritual death (Eph. 2:1,5). Regeneration is the point when this negative state of our souls is reversed. It is a new creation (2 Cor. 5:17) when we are inwardly renewed (Titus 3:5). It is a resurrection from death to new life (Eph. 2:5-6), new life in the kingdom of God's beloved Son (Col. 1:13).

Such a momentous act as new birth or regeneration cannot be accomplished by our own efforts; it is an act of God Himself upon the soul. God's prophetic word through Ezekiel makes it very clear that He alone is the author of this work: "Moreover, I will give you a new heart and put a new spirit within you; and I will remove the heart of stone from your flesh and give you a heart of flesh" (Ezek. 36:26). Specifically it is the work of the Holy Spirit, as the next words of Ezekiel's prophecy indicate:

> "I will give you a new heart and put a new spirit within you; and I will remove the heart of stone from your flesh and give you a heart of flesh."

"And I will put My Spirit within you and cause you to walk in My statutes" (Ezek. 36:27). In the words of John 3:5, we are "born of the Spirit." Paul calls it the "regeneration and renewing by the Holy Spirit" (Titus 3:5).

As was indicated above, this personal regeneration by the Spirit is a blessing that began on the day of Pentecost and is limited to those of the Christian era. Old Testament saints did not enjoy the

**37**

reality of the indwelling Spirit and His regenerating power. Thus in John 3:3-5 the reference was totally future as far as Nicodemus was concerned. The kingdom that he longed to enter was yet to be established, and the condition for entering it was not yet available. Nor was Christian baptism, which according to these words of Jesus was to be intimately associated with being born again into the kingdom.

## Baptism and Salvation

Given the probability that "water" in John 3:5 refers to Christian baptism, and given the fact that "born again" and "kingdom of God" refer to salvation, we cannot avoid the conclusion that baptism is inseparable from the new birth and thus is a condition for salvation. This is in full agreement with the teaching of Mark 16:16.

The declaration in John 3:5 is unmistakably clear. Unless a person is "born of water and the Spirit," he cannot enter the kingdom, that is, he cannot be saved. This new birth that must precede entrance into the kingdom is *ex* [*ek*] *hudatos kai pneumatos*, "from water and Spirit." The preposition *ek* basically means "from," either in the sense of separation ("away from") or source ("out of"). Only the latter fits the context here. In some sense, water and Spirit are the source of the new birth. Various shades of meaning as worded by Arndt and Gingrich include these; "the direction from which something comes," "origin," "effective cause," "the reason which is a presupposition for something," "the source from which something flows."[5]

These are very strong meanings, most of which reflect some type of cause-and-effect relationship. No one disputes such a meaning of *ek* when applied to *pneumatos* ("of Spirit"). That the Holy Spirit is the origin or source or cause of the new birth is accepted as very natural. Thus it is quite a jolt for some to recognize that the same preposition and the same grammatical form used for "Spirit" are used also for "water." It is a single prepositional phrase, with a single preposition which has two objects joined by the simple conjunction *kai* ("and"). Such a construction (especially the non-repetition of the preposition for the second object) brings the two objects into the closest possible relationship, marking them as two aspects of a single event. M.J. Harris makes the following comment concerning this construction and this verse:

> . . . Sometimes, therefore, the non-use of a second or third [preposition] in NT Gk. may be theologically significant, indicating that the writer regarded the terms that he placed in one regimen as belonging naturally together or as a unit in concept or reality, *ex hydatos kai pneumatos* (Jn. 3:5) shows that for the writer (or speaker) "water" and "Spirit" together form a single means of that regeneration which is a prerequisite for entrance into the kingdom of God. . . . No contrast is intended between an external element of "water" and an inward renewal achieved by the Spirit. Conceptually the two are one. . . .[6]

The whole expression, says Beasley-Murray, defines the manner in which a person is "born again" (verse 3).[7]

Does this mean that water and Spirit have an equal or identical causal relationship to the new birth? Few if any would be willing to go this far; metaphysical limitations simply preclude it. The only true source, cause, or origin of the new birth in any literal sense is the Holy Spirit. This is true not just because Spirit alone can impact upon spirit, but also because this birth is something that only God can accomplish. No physical act performed by a creature could do what only the Divine Spirit can do.

> The only true source, cause, or origin of the new birth in any literal sense is the Holy Spirit.

Nevertheless the language of John 3:5 makes the action of the Spirit *at least simultaneous* with the act of baptism. Thus the least that should be said is that baptism is the *occasion* for the new birth.[8] If anyone is dissatisfied with this terminology, it should only be because it is too weak, not too strong. The language of John 3:5 actually warrants a much stronger way of speaking of the relationship between baptism and salvation.[9]

This verse more than any other in Scripture shows the propriety of speaking of the *necessity* of baptism for salvation. As we saw in the discussion of Mark 16:16, however, this is only a *relative* necessity, not an absolute one. Just as the wording in Mark suggests that the only absolute necessity on man's part is faith, so does the wording in John suggest that only the working of the Spirit is absolutely necessary to accomplish the new birth (as compared with water). This is the conclusion some draw from John 3:6,8, where "born of the Spirit" is used but not "born of water." The action of the Spirit is the only thing absolutely indispensable for the new birth. Baptism is not inherently necessary and can be omitted where physically impossible to administer. The possibility of such an exception in prohibitive circumstances does not negate the rule laid down in John 3:5 for ordinary circumstances, however. Surely our doctrine of baptism must be based on clear statements concerning its nature and effects, and not on inferred exceptions.

## Summary

Concerning John 3:3-5 we have seen that the term *water* in verse 5 most probably is a reference to Christian baptism even though it was not instituted until later at Pentecost. We have seen also that this Pentecostal inception applies as well to the new birth and the establishment of the kingdom, which are concepts related to salvation in the Christian age. "Entering the kingdom" means receiving salvation, and "born again" is an essential condition for it. Finally we have seen that baptism itself is a (relative) necessity for salvation, since one cannot enter the kingdom without it.

### NOTES

1. A helpful discussion of this complaint is Donald Nash, "Water and Baptism," *Christian Standard* (April 30, 1978), 113:396-398.
2. Matt. 3:11,16; Mark 1:8,10; Luke 3:16; John 1:26,31,33; 3:23; Acts 1:5; 8:36,38,39; 10:47; 11:16.

3. John 4:10,11,14,15; 7:38.

4. John 1:13; 1 John 2:29; 3:9; 4:7; 5:1,4,18.

5. William F. Arndt and F. Wilbur Gingrich, *A Greek-English Lexicon of the New Testament and Other Early Christian Literature,* 4th ed. (Chicago: University of Chicago Press, 1952), 233-234.

6. Murray J. Harris, "Appendix," 1178.

7. Beasley-Murray, *Baptism in the New Testament,* 228, fn. 2. This, he says, is a reason why the reference to water cannot mean physical birth.

8. Beasley-Murray (ibid., 231) agrees: "In John 3:5 it is the occasion when the Spirit gives to faith the regeneration that qualifies for the Kingdom."

9. This is no doubt the reason why many will not admit that "water" means baptism in this verse. They have concluded on theological (rather than exegetical) grounds that baptism *cannot* have such a relationship to salvation.

# ~4~
# ACTS 2:38-39 (I)

robably the clearest — and probably for that reason the most controversial — passage concerning the meaning of baptism is Acts 2:38-39, "And Peter said to them, repent, and let each of you be baptized in the name of Jesus Christ for the forgiveness of your sins; and you shall receive the gift of the Holy Spirit. For the promise is for you and your children, and for all who are far off, as many as the Lord our God shall call to Himself.'" This passage is important because it describes the function of Christian baptism at the point of its very inauguration on the day of Pentecost. It is part of the apostolic instruction to sinners who are asking how they might be rid of their sin and guilt. It states quite clearly that baptism is the focal point of God's promises of forgiveness and the gift of the Spirit.

## The Messianic Outpouring of the Spirit

On the Jewish calendar the events of Acts 2 occurred on the day of Pentecost. To the Christian community the day is significant because it was the birthday of the church. On a deeper level still, it was the formal and historical point of transition from the Old Covenant age to the New Covenant age, the actual foundation for which had already been laid in the death and resurrection of Christ.

The central event marking the inauguration of the new age was the outpouring of the Holy Spirit. Of course the Holy Spirit was present and working among the saints of God in Old Testament

> The central event marking the inauguration of the new age was the outpouring of the Holy Spirit.

times, but both the prophets and the Gospels promised a new and special presence of the Spirit as part of the Messianic hope. Isaiah 44:3 says, "For I will pour out water on the thirsty land and streams on the dry ground; I will pour out My Spirit on your offspring, and My blessing on your descendants." Joel 2:28 says, "And it will come about after this that I will pour out My Spirit on all mankind." Ezekiel 36:27 puts it thus: "And I will put My Spirit within you and cause you to walk in My statutes." John the Baptist promised that the Messiah would baptize with the Holy Spirit (Matt. 3:11; Mark 1:7-8; Luke 3:16; John 1:33). Jesus promised that the Spirit would be given to believers as an indwelling presence (Luke 11:13; John 7:37-39). At His ascension He renewed this promise, as recorded in Acts 1:4-8. He told His apostles to "wait for what the Father had promised."

The activities recorded in Acts 2:1-4 are the initial fulfilment of these promises. The outward, miraculous manifestations were not the main point of Pentecost, but only the signs or evidence that the invisible, inner presence of the Spirit was now available for the first time.[1] The miracles — especially the speaking with "other tongues" (Acts 2:4) — succeeded in their purpose of gaining the attention of the crowd and disposing them toward the message Peter was to deliver. The people asked in amazement, "What does this mean?" (Acts 2:12). Peter proceeded to explain what it meant. This is the outpouring of the Spirit promised by Joel, he said. It is one of the primary blessings of the accomplished work of Jesus the Messiah. You crucified Him, said Peter to the Jews assembled there, but God raised Him from the dead and seated Him at His own right hand. "And having received from the Father the promise of the Holy Spirit, He has poured forth this which you both see and hear" (Acts 2:33). For this Jesus whom you crucified has been exalted as your Lord and Christ (Acts 2:15-36).

The audience that heard Peter's sermon was a large group of devout Jews who worshiped God according to the Old Covenant revelation. No doubt many of them had encountered Jesus and rejected Him, thinking they were defending Jahweh's honor. What they heard from Peter, as confirmed by the miraculous manifestations of the Spirit, shook them to the very foundations of their faith. Jesus — whom they had sent to His death — was their God-sent, God-exalted Messiah! From His heavenly throne, as the inaugural expression of His Lordship, He had sent forth the long-awaited Holy Spirit! When this realization dawned upon them, they sensed themselves as sinners exposed to the wrath of God. "They were pierced to the heart, and said to Peter and the rest of the apostles, 'Brethren, what shall we do?'" (Acts 2:37).

"What shall we do" about what? About their burden of sin and guilt. What could they do to be free of this burden? Here is a primary example of the point made earlier while discussing Matthew 28, that even the most faithful Jews, when confronted with the new revelation of the gospel of Christ, became lost sinners unless and until they accepted Jesus as their Savior and Messiah. Peter's audience now felt this state of lostness and cried out for help. "What shall we do" to be saved?

Peter's statement concerning baptism in Acts 2:38-39 must be understood against this background. Baptism is at the very heart of his answer to the question about what must be done to be free from sin and guilt.

## The Gospel Offer

Peter's reply to the sinners' question may be analyzed in two parts: first, the nature of the salvation offered; and second, the conditions for receiving it.

The gospel offer made here in Acts 2:38 is a classic representation of the "double cure" referred to in the song "Rock of Ages," viz., "Be of sin the double cure; save me from its guilt and power." An alternative version says, "Save from wrath and make me pure." This double cure is God's answer to the "double trouble" sinners bring upon themselves through their sin.[2]

**45**

The first and most immediately pressing problem caused by sin is *guilt*. The sinner has broken God's law and thus has incurred its penalty. He stands under the constant condemnation of the wrath of God. This is an objective problem, a problem of wrong relationships with God and with His law. God's solution to man's guilt is the death of Christ, in which He took our sin with its guilt upon Himself, paying its penalty through His own suffering. As a result God is able to offer the sinner full pardon for his sin, full remission, complete justification, complete liberation from the fear of condemnation and hell.

This is "the forgiveness of your sins" that Peter offers in Acts 2:38, and it is no doubt what his Jewish audience was inquiring about. Forgiveness itself is not a new blessing of the Messianic age, but was enjoyed by all believers in the pre-Christian era also. The newness is that now it is offered only "in the name of Jesus Christ" since His death and resurrection are the events that make it possible in the first place. In any case Peter's offer included first of all what was most wanted and most needed by his audience.

The second part of the double trouble is not as readily perceived and understood as the first. It is the effect that sin has on the soul itself. It can be described as sinfulness, depravity, spiritual weakness, spiritual sickness, even spiritual death. The vitiating effects of sin permeate the soul just as the ravages of disease permeate the body; they make the soul weak in the face of temptation and inclined to sin more and more. In other words, sin affects not just our *relationship* to God and His law; it also affects us *personally*. Our very nature is corrupted.

> The gospel offer to sinners in the Christian era includes a divine cure for this disease of the soul.

The gospel offer to sinners in the Christian era includes a divine cure for this disease of the soul. It is the new birth or regeneration, as discussed earlier in connection with John 3:3-5. As noted there, this was not made available to sinners in the Old Testament era. Though they were provided with some resources to combat the power of sin, still they were not given the gift of rebirth. This is one of the principal new blessings of the Messianic age and one of the main aspects of the gospel offer. Thus the Jews who asked "Brethren, what shall we do?" probably were not even aware of this side of the sin problem and thus were not asking about any solution to it. So when Peter's offer included the words, "and you shall receive the gift of the Holy Spirit," this was an unexpected bonus! For "the gift of the Holy Spirit" is the person and presence of the Spirit Himself, who will enter the receptive sinner's heart in order to regenerate him and will remain there in order to give him strength to overcome sin day by day. The offer of the Holy Spirit *is* the offer of regeneration.

This was Peter's ultimate explanation of the tongues and other phenomena recorded in Acts 2:1-4 and about which the audience originally asked, "What does this mean?" (Acts 2:12). What this means, says Peter, is that God through Christ has now poured out the promised Spirit. And what it means *for you* is that, if you will repent and be baptized in the name of Christ for the remission of your sins, *you* will receive this very Holy Spirit as a gift. For the promised Spirit *is for you* (Acts 2:39; the word order makes the "you" emphatic).

## The Conditions

As is the case in Mark 16:16, the gospel offer in Acts 2:38 is conditional. A large segment of conservative Protestantism teaches that God's gracious salvation is completely unconditional, but this view is based on a faulty view of divine sovereignty and some questionable exegesis.[3] Scripture clearly connects the sinner's reception of salvation with his meeting of certain basic conditions. In Mark 16:16 faith and baptism are specified; here in Acts 2:38 repentance and baptism are specifically mentioned.

When his Jewish brethren asked, "What shall we do?" Peter's first instruction was that they should *repent*. Repentance as a condition for salvation is not a controversial point, even among those who like to emphasize "faith alone." It is generally recognized

**47**

that the faith which God requires for salvation cannot really exist without repentance. The latter is basically an attitude toward *sin*. It is a hatred of sin in general and especially a hatred of the sin in one's own life; it is a determination and commitment to be rid of all sin as quickly as possible. Since the holy God Himself hates sin, one cannot truly believe in Him without sharing this hatred. Since Christ's very purpose and work was to oppose and conquer sin in all its forces and forms, and since His very blood was shed to accomplish this, one cannot truly believe in Christ without hating the sin which caused His suffering. Thus even in passages where it is not specified (as in Acts 16:31), it is understood that repentance is the Siamese twin or silent partner of faith.

In Acts 2:38 repentance is the first condition mentioned because the thing foremost in the minds of those who heard Peter's sermon was the conviction of their sin, especially their sin of rejecting Christ and causing His death. Their question specifically meant, "What shall we do *about these terrible sins*?" First, says Peter, you must have the right attitude toward them: you must repent.

The only other condition given by Peter is baptism: "Let each of you be baptized in the name of Jesus Christ for the forgiveness of your sins." Since Mark lists baptism as a condition for salvation, and since John gives it as a condition for entrance into the kingdom of God, we should not be surprised that it is presented here as a condition for the forgiveness of sins, as well as for receiving the gift of the Spirit.

Of course many do find it difficult to accept what Peter says about baptism and look for ways to avoid its implications. One such way is to deny that Acts 2:38 refers to *water* baptism. As one writer says, "I doubt very seriously whether Peter was referring to water baptism," because there would not have been enough water in the temple area to immerse 3,000 people (Acts 2:41) and because neither here nor anywhere else is *water* baptism specifically connected with the forgiveness of sins.[4]

> Many do find it difficult to accept what Peter says about baptism and look for ways to avoid its implications.

Such an idea is not very well thought out, however. Peter must have meant water baptism for the following reasons. First, he must have been speaking of the same baptism prescribed in the Great Commission, which had to be water baptism because it was something the apostles themselves were to administer. Second, the baptism prescribed by Peter was something the sinners themselves were to do ("What shall *we* do?"); it was their decision and initiative. A purely *spiritual* baptism would be at God's initiative. Third, Peter's language would have immediately called to his audience's mind the baptism of John (which was "a baptism of *repentance* for the *forgiveness of sins*," Mark 1:4), which was known to all as water baptism. Finally it should be noted that there was ample water in the Jerusalem area (it did not have to be in the *temple* area) for immersing 3,000 people.[5]

Thus there is no good reason for seeing this as a reference to anything besides water baptism. It is set forth alongside repentance as a condition for receiving the blessings of salvation. This should not be surprising in view of the prominence of baptism in the Great Commission as reported by both Matthew and Mark. In fact, it would have been surprising if Peter had *not* mentioned baptism when asked, "What shall we do?"

This leads to a final consideration relative to the conditions specified in Acts 2:38, namely, why *is faith* not included here, especially since the commission in Mark 16:16 includes both faith and baptism? We could infer from both the question in Acts 2:37 and the reply in Acts 2:38 that it was not necessary to specify faith since those who heard the message and were "pierced to the heart" by it (verse 37) *already believed*. This is why they asked for further instruction on what to do. If Peter had perceived that they did not yet believe, he surely would have required this first of all.

This may be compared with the situation in Acts 16:30-31, when the Philippian jailer asked basically the same question, "What must I do to be saved?" This man, a pagan, had not as yet had the benefit of hearing a message about the true God or our Lord Jesus Christ. Thus Paul's reply focused on the foundational requirement: "Believe in the Lord Jesus, and you shall be saved." This instruction was not meant to be comprehensive and all-inclusive; it was an opening statement immediately followed by more teaching: "And they spoke the word of the Lord to him" (Acts 16:32). Though neither repentance nor baptism is specifically mentioned, we can fairly infer that they were included in this "word of the Lord." This is surely the case with baptism, since the jailer was immediately baptized after hearing the teaching (Acts 16:33).

In a similar way we can consider Peter's instruction in Acts 2:38 to have been determined by the level of response already achieved by his hearers. Since a measure of faith was already evidenced by their question, there was no need to mention it specifically.

In this connection one other point may be noted. Even though faith is not specifically mentioned here as a condition for salvation, the content of Peter's reply was an *implicit* call for faith, and not just the faith of Old Testament saints. It was a call for these devout Jews to rise to a new level of faith, to focus their faith upon a God who is Three as well as One. As we noted in the discussion of Matthew 28:19-20, from this time forward saving faith must include faith in Jesus as the divine Redeemer and faith in the Holy Spirit as the divine gift. A conscientious response to Peter's instruction would have to include these elements, since he told this group to be baptized *in the name of Jesus Christ* in order to *receive the gift of the Holy Spirit*. Their Old Covenant faith was no longer adequate; whether they had been baptized with John's baptism was now irrelevant. They are now required to accept God's word about Jesus Christ and the Spirit as part of their acceptance of baptism itself.

> The content of Peter's reply was an implicit call for faith.

In summary, then, the conditions for receiving the "double cure" according to Acts 2:38 are repentance and baptism, plus an implied faith.

## NOTES

1. See Jack Cottrell, "Are Miraculous Gifts the Blessing of Pentecost?" *Christian Standard* (May 9, 1982), 117:9-11.

2. See Jack Cottrell, *Thirteen Lessons on Grace: Being Good Enough Isn't Good Enough* (Joplin, Mo.: College Press, 1988 reprint of 1976 edition published by Standard Publishing), chs. 5-7.

3. See Jack Cottrell, *What the Bible Says About God the Ruler* (Joplin, Mo.: College Press, 1984), chs. 5, 9; and *What the Bible Says About God the Redeemer,* 389-399.

4. Richard A. Seymour, *All About Repentance* (Hollywood, Fla.: Harvest House, 1974), 123. The last point of course is a case of begging the question.

5. Several large pools were available, such as the Pool of Siloam (just south of the temple area), which measures approximately 15 by 50 feet. A large reservoir on the southwest side of the city had a surface area of about 3 acres. See J.W. McGarvey, *Lands of the Bible* (Philadelphia: Lippincott, 1881), 189-202, for a full description of the pools of Jerusalem.

# ~5~
# ACTS 2:38-39 (II)

In chapter four above we noted that in Acts 2:38-39 Peter specifies two conditions for receiving the gospel blessings of forgiveness and the Holy Spirit, namely, repentance and baptism. In this chapter we will explore in more detail how baptism is related to each of these blessings.

## Baptism and Forgiveness

Baptism for the forgiveness of sins in the Christian age is not without antecedents in the previous era. It was foreshadowed by the Old Testament ritual purification ceremonies, also called lustrations or washings.

In the context of the Mosaic law, some acts and conditions produced a state of ritual or ceremonial uncleanness, e.g., having certain bodily discharges (Lev. 15) and touching a corpse (Num. 19:11-22). The state of uncleanness produced thereby was not moral in nature, but ritual or ceremonial. No moral fault of guilt was attached; some of the situations causing it were natural and unavoidable. The principal effect was that the person rendered unclean was considered unfit to engage in the religious services before God. To remove such defilement, certain purification rites were prescribed, most of them involving water (e.g., Lev. 11:32; 14:8; Deut. 23:10-11).

On certain occasions and for worship leaders especially, water purification was required before one could approach God even when no specific offense was in view. See Exodus 19:10,14; 29:4;

Lev. 16:4. The bronze laver used for priestly washing was particularly significant. The ministering priests were required to wash therein before serving in the tabernacle; "they shall wash with water, that they may not die" (Exod. 30:20).

In what sense did the water or the act itself have such a dramatic effect or bring about purification? The fact is that neither the water nor the act of washing *caused* any change. It was a matter of divine decision and declaration. God simply declared that before the act of washing, the person was unacceptable in His sight; afterwards the person was regarded as acceptable.

If the state of uncleanness and the washing rites themselves had only a ceremonial significance, then what was the purpose of this whole system? Basically it had a symbolic or typical purpose. The whole system of *ceremonial* uncleanness and purification was an object lesson to teach about *moral* pollution and true *legal* guilt before God, and the necessity of the heart's being cleansed from these. This is how the prophets made use of the ceremonies in their teaching. They used the ritual cleansings as analogies of the moral cleansing with which God is especially concerned. Typical teaching involving this conceptual transition from ritual to moral includes Psalm 51:2,7, "Wash me thoroughly from my iniquity, and cleanse me from my sin. . . . Wash me, and I shall be whiter than snow"; Isaiah 1:16, "Wash yourselves, make yourselves clean; remove the evil of your deeds from My sight"; Jeremiah 4:14, "Wash your heart from evil, O Jerusalem, that you may be saved"; and Ezekiel 36:25, "Then I will sprinkle clean water on you, and you will be clean; I will cleanse you from all your filthiness and from all your idols."

The Old Testament water ceremonies, together with the prophetic imagery of divine spiritual cleansing, are the forerunners of Christian baptism. The latter unites outward washing and inner moral cleansing into a single act, viz., baptism for the forgiveness of sins. Baptism is to moral and spiritual defilement what the Old Testament washings were to ritual defilement.

> Baptism is to moral and spiritual defilement what the Old Testament washings were to ritual defilement.

John the Baptist's baptism also had a connection with forgiveness, though it is never stated in the same terms as Christian baptism. It was a baptism "for repentance" (Matt. 3:11), "a baptism of repentance for the forgiveness of sins" (Mark 1:4; Luke 3:3). Those who were baptized confessed their sins in the process (Matt. 3:6; Mark 1:5). Thus repentance, confession of sin, and forgiveness of sin were all related to John's baptism. Whether the baptism was preached as a condition for this forgiveness or whether it was only an aid to quicken and intensify repentance is not clear.

The relation between Christian baptism and forgiveness of sins is much more specific and clear, though, especially here in Acts 2:38, where baptism is said to be "for [*eis*] the forgiveness of sins." The key word here is *eis*, translated in different versions in a wide variety of ways including "for," "unto," "into," "in order to," "in order to have," "so that," "with a view to," and "in relation to." The preferred terminology is a matter of considerable controversy since exegetes often try to make the word conform to a preconceived view of baptism.

Three main approaches may be identified. The first is that *eis* here retains its most common meaning of *direction or motion toward something*, which includes the concepts of *purpose* and *goal*. On this understanding the purpose or goal of baptism is to bring about forgiveness of sins. This view is consistent with the idea of baptism as a condition for salvation and for entrance into the kingdom of God. A second approach is that *eis* here means *because of*, the idea being that a person is baptized because his sins have already been forgiven. The third view is that *eis* here means the same thing as the preposition *en* ("in"), which does not mean motion toward but simply *location in*. This view posits only a very general connection between baptism and forgiveness, viz., "be baptized *in relation to* forgiveness of sins." The last two views are preferred by those who reject the conditional relation between baptism and salvation.

Of these three views, the first is clearly the meaning in Acts 2:38 on both lexicographical and contextual grounds. Regarding

**55**

its actual meaning, a study of the lexicons shows that the primary meaning and the overwhelmingly most common use of *eis* is "motion toward" in any one of a number of senses, the explanation of which takes two full pages in the Arndt and Gingrich lexicon.[1] In this general category the two most common meanings are "moving from one physical place to another" (88 lines in the lexicon) and "goal or purpose" (127 lines — one full page). By contrast only five lines are devoted to the alleged causal use of *eis*. Arndt and Gingrich call this use "controversial" because there is reason to doubt that it ever has this meaning in Greek usage.[2] M.J. Harris flatly declares that this causal sense "seems unlikely in any one of the passages sometimes adduced," including Acts 2:38.[3] A meaning similar to that of *en* is not disputed but is still relatively infrequent. Arndt and Gingrich use only 16 lines to explain that *eis* sometimes means "with respect to" or "with reference to." Most of the cases where *eis* is used where *en* would be expected (30 of 34 lines) refer to physical location.[4]

Of course it is understood that simply counting lines in a lexicon does not decide the meaning of a word in a particular verse. The point is to show that the primary meaning of *eis* involves motion toward or purpose, and that this is how it is used in the overwhelming majority of cases. The meaning "because of" is highly debatable simply because it has no solid basis in the Greek language as such. The meaning "with reference to" is possible but not as likely given its relatively infrequent use. Thus if *eis* has one of these last two meanings in Acts 2:38, that meaning would have to be contextually clear.

In the final analysis the meaning of *eis* in this passage will be determined by the context. The general meaning "with reference to" would be warranted only if the context itself did not suggest a more specific meaning, only if the connection between baptism and forgiveness remained vague in the context. But this is certainly not the case. We must remember that Peter's statement is part of his answer to the Jews' question of how to get rid of the guilt of their sins, especially their sin of crucifying Christ. They specifically asked, "What shall we do" to get rid of this guilt? Any instruction Peter gave them would have been understood by them in this light, and must be so understood by us today. When he told them to repent and be baptized *"eis* the forgiveness" of their sins, the only honest reading is that baptism is for the *purpose* or *goal* of receiving forgiveness. This meaning is not just warranted but is actually demanded by the context.

> The only honest reading is that baptism is for the purpose or goal of receiving forgiveness.

The fact that baptism is paralleled here with repentance confirms this meaning. Surely no one questions that Peter is telling his audience to repent for the purpose of bringing about forgiveness of sins. Even if such a connection between repentance and forgiveness were not already understood, it is perfectly unambiguous in this context. The fact that baptism is part of the same response to the same question makes its meaning just as clear and gives it the same basic meaning as repentance. In whatever way repentance is connected with forgiveness, so also is baptism. If repentance is for the purpose of bringing about forgiveness, so also is baptism.

Even if the so-called "causal" meaning of *eis* were not in doubt on lexicographical grounds, it would surely be excluded in Acts 2:38 by the context itself. "Be baptized because your sins have been forgiven" is the exact opposite of what would be expected and required in the situation. The whole point is that the Jews' sins are *not* forgiven, and they are asking what to do to receive such forgiveness.

The bottom line is that the only meaning of *eis* that is consistent with the context of Acts 2:38 is its most common meaning of "motion toward," specifically the purposive meaning of "unto" or "for the purpose of." The Greek construction is exactly the same as Jesus' statement in Matthew 26:28, that he shed his blood "for [*eis*] forgiveness of sins," namely, for the purpose of bringing about forgiveness. Thus we must conclude that Peter is saying in Acts 2:38 that part of what a sinner must do to bring about forgiveness of his sins is be baptized.

One other point must be made concerning the relation between baptism and forgiveness. Quite often we hear that a person is baptized "for the forgiveness of his *past* sins." Sometimes the language of Romans 3:25 (KJV) is taken out of context and applied here, viz., that a person is baptized "for the remission of sins that are past." The idea is that baptism brings forgiveness for every sin committed up to that point, and that a person thus remains completely forgiven until he sins again. Then he reverts to a state of lostness because of the newly committed sin, and remains in this state until some further forgiving act is performed, such as partaking of the Lord's Supper or making specific confession of such sin (1 John 1:9). Such thinking underlies the development of the Roman Catholic sacrament of penance.

Such thinking is false, however, and is based on a faulty concept not only of baptism but of forgiveness itself. The forgiveness of sins is in essence the same as justification (cf. Romans 3:28; 4:6-8). When one receives forgiveness in baptism, he becomes a justified or forgiven person. He enters the state of being justified. This is a continuing state that is maintained through continuing faith in the blood of Jesus.[5] Through his sincere and working faith a Christian remains free from guilt and condemnation (Rom. 8:1) even if he is not free from sin itself. This is the heart of the concept of justification by faith.

This means that baptism is not for the forgiveness of past sins only, but for the forgiveness of sins, *period*. As long as one remains in the relationship to Christ begun at baptism, he is justified or forgiven as the result of what happened in his baptism. Thus all our lives we should remember our baptism, and be encouraged by that memory when we begin to feel discouraged in our Christian living or to doubt the validity of our hope in Christ Jesus.

> Baptism is not for the forgiveness of past sins only, but for the forgiveness of sins, period.

## Baptism and the Holy Spirit

In our study of John 3:5 we have already seen that there is a close relationship between baptism and the Holy Spirit, in that both are related to the new birth. Here in Acts 2:38 that connection is made even stronger and more specific. The gift of the Spirit Himself as an indwelling presence is promised as the result of Christian baptism: "Be baptized in the name of Jesus Christ for the forgiveness of your sins; and you shall receive the gift of the Holy Spirit."

The reality of the inner presence of the Spirit in our very lives and bodies is a fact taught forcefully and clearly in Scripture. See Romans 8:9-11; 1 Corinthians 6:19; 2 Timothy 1:14. Acts 2:38 tells us that baptism is the point of time when the Spirit enters our lives in this way.[6]

Though baptism is a single act involving both water and Spirit (John 3:5), this passage shows that baptism in water actually precedes or is a precondition for the Spirit's regenerating work accomplished therein. In baptism the Holy Spirit is given; He then gives the new birth by His very presence. Thus, although they are for the most part simultaneous, technically they do not begin at the same time.

As suggested earlier in this chapter, the gift of the indwelling Spirit is the very heart of the Pentecost message and promise. Before His ascension Jesus told His apostles to wait in Jerusalem for "what the Father had promised" (Acts 1:4-5). The phenomena of Pentecost confirmed that this promise was fulfilled on that day (Acts 2:16-17,33); from that time forward the

> The gift of the indwelling Spirit is the very heart of the Pentecost message and promise.

gift of the Spirit has been offered to anyone who repents and is baptized in the name of Jesus (Acts 2:38-39). Thus as unlikely as it may seem, this long-promised and long-expected gift of inestimable value is by God's design made to depend on baptism! This is indicated in Acts 5:32 also, where Peter notes that God has given the Holy Spirit "to those who obey Him" — an obvious reference to Acts 2:38. From this alone we can see what an important place God has assigned to baptism in the economy of salvation.

A problem is raised by the fact that on several occasions in the book of Acts the Holy Spirit seems to be given apart from baptism, either before it or after it. Some conclude from these events that the giving of the Spirit follows no set pattern and especially that it has no particular connection with baptism.

Twice the Holy Spirit is given *before* baptism, namely, at Pentecost (Acts 2:1-4) and at the conversion of Cornelius and his household (Acts 10:44-48). It is a serious mistake, however, to see these events as typical and as representative conversion experiences. In fact, they are intended to be just the opposite. In the first place, it is not clear whether the pre-baptismal presence of the Spirit in these cases resulted in conversion (the new birth) at all, or whether it was simply a matter of equipping these particular individuals with the miraculous ability to speak in tongues.

In the second place, even if they did involve the new birth, the evidential purposes of these two events required them to be unusual and unique and contrary to the normal pattern of conversion. In each case the main point was the miraculous tongues, which functioned as signs of the truth of the apostolic testimony. At Pentecost the tongues established the message that this was the beginning of the new-age outpouring of the Spirit. In Acts 10 the tongues were evidence that God wanted the Gentiles to be received into His church along with the Jews. Thus these events were not intended to be paradigms of conversion. They were meant to be exceptions to the rule in the sense that every miracle is an exception; this is what gives them their evidential value.

In the third place, Peter specifically indicates that the manner of the Spirit's coming at Pentecost and upon Cornelius stood apart from the normal experience. He notes that Cornelius and his household "received the Holy Spirit just as we did" (Acts 10:47; cf. 15:8), but Acts 11:15 shows that he regards the *manner* in which they received Him to be comparable only to the Pentecost experience itself: "And as I began to speak, the Holy Spirit fell upon them, just as He did upon us at the beginning." And what was the unique thing about these two occasions? These are the only two recorded cases where the Spirit was given without any human intermediary of any kind, where the Spirit *immediately* fell upon the chosen individuals. In every other case a human mediator is involved, either through baptism or the laying on of hands.

The conclusion is that Acts 2:1-4 and Acts 10:44-48 do not negate the truth of Acts 2:38 concerning the appointed connection between baptism and the Holy Spirit. They give no warrant whatsoever for expecting the Spirit to be given prior to baptism.

On two other occasions in the book of Acts, however, the Spirit seems to be given *after* baptism, in the separate action of the laying on of an apostle's hands: see Acts 8:17-18; 19:6. The assumption that these two passages refer to the gift of the indwelling Spirit is one reason for the rise of the practice of confirmation in some church groups. But that is the question: is the giving of the Spirit in these two cases the same as that promised in Acts 2:38? It seems not to be.

What sets these two events apart from the normal conversion experience in which the indwelling Spirit is given in Christian baptism? Basically, they both appear to involve not the indwelling of the Spirit but the bestowing of *miraculous gifts* of the Spirit. At Samaria what was bestowed through the laying on of the apostles' hands was something observable and awesome (Acts 8:18); in Acts 19:6 the result is specifically given as "speaking with tongues and prophesying." Especially from the account of Philip's mission in Samaria (Acts 8:5-18), we are justified in concluding that miraculous spiritual gifts could be bestowed only through the laying on of an apostle's hands. (This is why the Pentecost and Cornelius events were unique: even the *manner* in which the miraculous abilities were given was a miracle.) Because of the unqualified promise in Acts 2:38 (cf. Acts 5:32), we may thus conclude that both the Samaritan disciples and the Ephesian disciples received the indwelling of the Spirit when they were baptized (Acts 8:12; 19:5); subsequently they were given miraculous spiritual gifts when the apostles laid their hands on them.

Again the connection between baptism and the Holy Spirit established in Acts 2:38 remains unshaken. Events which depart from this pattern are either deliberately unique or are referring to something other than the gift of the indwelling Spirit that provides the new birth. This understanding is consistent with the testimony of other New Testament passages which tie baptism to the regenerating work of the Spirit, viz., John 3:5; Romans 6:3ff; Colossians 2:12; and Titus 3:5.

# Summary

In this chapter and the one preceding we have sought to explain the meaning of baptism as found in Peter's instruction in Acts 2:38-39. We have emphasized the significance of the historical context, namely, that this was the day when God gave the long-awaited Messianic outpouring of the Holy Spirit. This was also the occasion when the Jews were confronted with their guilt of rejecting and crucifying Christ, who was confirmed as their Messiah by His resurrection and enthronement and by His participation in the sending of the Spirit. Thousands in Peter's audience came under conviction and asked what they could do to be free from the guilt of their sin.

We have seen that Peter's response included the promise of a "double cure" from the "double trouble" of sin: forgiveness to remove their guilt, and the indwelling Holy Spirit to give them a new birth to new spiritual life. His response also included the conditions for receiving these blessings: repentance and baptism.

> Peter's response included the promise of a "double cure" from the "double trouble" of sin.

We have discussed in some detail the connection between baptism and forgiveness as stated here in Acts 2:38. Of special significance is the use of the Greek word *eis*, which is shown by lexical considerations and by the context to mean "unto" or "for the purpose of." Thus the very purpose of baptism is to bring about forgiveness or justification.

Finally we have discussed the connection between baptism and the Holy Spirit, emphasizing that baptism is a clear precondition for receiving the gift of the regenerating and indwelling presence of the Spirit. Passages in Acts which separate baptism from the gift of the Spirit are deliberately unique exceptions or are not talking about the saving presence of the Spirit in the first place.

## NOTES

1. Arndt and Gingrich, 227-229.
2. Ibid., 229. See the references to the debate in *The Journal of Biblical Literature*.
3. Murray J. Harris, "Appendix," 1187.
4. Arndt and Gingrich, 229.
5. It is possible for a person to lose his faith, in which case he would also lose his justification.
6. This giving of the Spirit is described as God's placing his *seal* of ownership upon us: "Having also believed, you were sealed in Him with the Holy Spirit of promise" (Eph. 1:13; cf. Eph. 4:30). Although the noun is not used in this context, the Spirit himself is undoubtedly the seal or mark of God's ownership. Contrary to much popular thinking, baptism as such is never called a seal. Rather, as Acts 2:38 shows, it is the *occasion* for the bestowing of the true seal, the Holy Spirit.

# ≈6≈
# ACTS 22:16

aptism is mentioned a number of times in the book of Acts after 2:38, but mostly just to record the fact that certain individuals were baptized (e.g., 8:12,38; 9:18; 10:48; 16:15,33). Only one other passage reflects significantly on the actual *meaning* of baptism, viz.. Acts 22:16. Here God's servant Ananias addresses the humbled Saul of Tarsus (who is about to become Paul the Apostle) with these words: "And now why do you delay? Arise, and be baptized, and wash away your sins, calling on His name."

## Saul the Sinner

To understand the meaning of baptism as taught in this passage, again we must study the historical context in which the statement is made. Especially we must inquire concerning Saul's spiritual state at the time Ananias addresses him. Is he already saved, or is he still an unsaved sinner? To find the answer we must study all three accounts of Saul's conversion together: Acts 9:1-19; 22:1-16; and 26:1-18.

Before his conversion experience Saul considered himself to be among the elite in believing Israel, a devout Jew who was "zealous for God" (22:3). From his perspective as a Christian, however, he realized that he had been the foremost sinner (1 Tim. 1:15). He was guilty of blasphemy, persecution of Christians and of Christ Himself (26:14-15), violence, and unbelief (1 Tim.

> Before his conversion experience Saul considered himself to be among the elite in believing Israel.

1:13). This is another example of how even the most sincere Old Covenant faith was no longer sufficient once Christ was known.

While Saul was on his way to Damascus to persecute more Christians, the risen and living Christ appeared to him and demanded, "Saul, why are you persecuting me?" The bewildered and bedazzled Saul could only ask, "Who are you, Lord?" The reply: "I am Jesus, the one you are actually persecuting" (9:5; 22:8; 26:15). Immediately filled with a sense of his guilt and with fear, Saul could only ask, "What shall I do, Lord?" The reply: "Go on in to Damascus, and there someone will tell you what to do" (22:10).

Blinded by the brilliance of the risen Christ, Saul was led into Damascus; but no one came to him for three days. During this time the blind Saul prayed and fasted, waiting for someone to help him. He knew from a vision that a man named Ananias would come for this purpose (9:9-12). Ananias, himself prepared by a vision, finally arrived after the three days of fasting and prayer. First he laid his hands on Saul so that the latter's sight might be miraculously restored (9:12,17-18; 22:13). Then he announced why the Lord had confronted Saul in such a radical way, namely, because He had chosen him to be an apostle to the Gentiles (22:14-15; see 9:15-16).[1] Finally, Ananias told Saul what to do about his sin and guilt: "Arise, and be baptized, and wash away your sins, calling on His name" (22:16).

Now the crucial question is this: can we discern whether Saul is still in his sins when thus exhorted, or whether he has already been saved? To put it another way, is there any point prior to this where he might have been fully converted?

Someone might suggest that he was converted on the Damascus road at the time of his encounter with Christ. Since he calls Jesus "Lord" (22:8,10), perhaps this means that he was at that point surrendering to the Lordship of Christ. This is unlikely, however. The word itself (Greek, *kurios)* was the usual term of respectful address, on which occasions it was roughly equivalent to our word "sir." Perhaps this is all Saul meant in his first use of this term, since at this point he does not even know who Jesus is:

"Who art Thou, Lord?" (22:8). But after Jesus identifies Himself (22:8), Saul again calls Him "Lord" (22:10), perhaps in a stronger sense than before, and perhaps even indicating an attitude of submission. It is still unlikely, though, that any true conversion has taken place. Saul had not yet heard the gospel offer, nor had he been told the conditions for receiving what is offered. This is why he asks, "What shall I do, Lord?" (22:10).

The fact that Saul asked this question suggests that he was at that time in the same spiritual condition as the Jews who were convicted by Peter's Pentecost sermon. They asked, "What shall we do?" (Acts 2:37). Saul's question is exactly the same:

"What shall I do?" But whereas they were immediately told how to receive forgiveness, Saul was not told at this point what to do about his sins. Thus we conclude that he is still in them here on the Damascus road.

But even if this is so, someone might say that Saul was surely converted during the three days when he was fasting and praying. But there is no indication that any change took place in him during this time. Conversion is usually accompanied by a deep sense of joy and relief (see Acts 8:39; 16:34), but this is not mentioned here. The fact that Saul continues to pray and fast during the whole three days shows he has not yet received that for which he is praying and fasting. He has still not had his question answered: "What shall I do?" He knows that someone named Ananias will come and tell him what to do (9:6,12), but nothing happens for three days. During this time he is still in his blindness, which is symbolic of the fact that he is still in his sins.

When Ananias first encounters Saul, what does he assume about the latter's spiritual condition? The fact that he addresses him as "Brother Saul" (9:17; 22:13) is taken by many to be a sure indication that Ananias accepts him as a fellow Christian and thus as a saved person. It is true that Christians called each other "brother" and "brethren." About 30 instances occur in Acts and 130 in Paul's own writings. But this practice probably arose from the fact that the *Jews* already customarily called each other "brethren,"[2] by which they meant only "fellow Jews." This is the sense in which Paul refers to all Jews as "my brethren, my kinsmen according to the flesh" (Rom. 9:3). The addressing of fellow Jews as brethren occurs quite often in the book of Acts;[3] thus we need not think that anything more than this is implied by Ananias's address of Saul as "brother."

In fact there are two strong indications that Ananias did not view Saul as a saved Christian brother when he first encountered him. As we have seen in our study of Acts 2:38, salvation in the Messianic age includes receiving the Holy Spirit. But Ananias says that he has been sent to Saul for the very purpose of filling him with the Holy Spirit (9:17). This shows that Saul was not yet saved, and that Ananias was quite aware of it. The other element of the double cure of salvation is forgiveness of sins. Now, when Ananias tells Saul to rise up and wash away his sins (22:16), this shows that he sees Saul as still bearing the burden of his guilt.

Thus there is nothing in the text or context that places Saul in the company of the saved when he first meets Ananias. He welcomes Ananias as the one whom God has sent at last to tell him what to do to be saved, and baptism is a central element in the instruction. It is related both to receiving the Spirit and to forgiveness, just as in Acts 2:38.

We can infer its relation to the Spirit in Saul's case from Acts 9:12,17-18. In verse 17 Ananias mentions two reasons why he was sent: that Saul might regain his sight and be filled with the Spirit. In the very next verse we are told that Saul's sight returned (when Ananias laid his hands on him, v. 12) *and* that he was baptized. The implication is that the latter was the occasion for the giving of the Spirit, as promised in Acts 2:38.

The relation of baptism to the forgiveness of Saul's sins is the focal point of Acts 22:16. We now turn to a more detailed study of this aspect of the verse.

> **The relation of baptism to the forgiveness of Saul's sins is the focal point of Acts 22:16.**

# Wash away Your Sins

Ananias's instruction to Saul includes two aorist participles, "rising up" and "calling upon"; and two imperatives, "be baptized" and "wash away your sins." This last item is the crucial one. What does it mean to "wash away" sins? At first the imagery might suggest to our minds the second part of the double cure, or the cleansing of our souls from the condition of sinfulness, a purifying change wrought within our very hearts. But this is not the main idea. It rather refers to the first part of the double cure, namely, the washing away of the *guilt* we have incurred because of our sins. It is equivalent to the forgiveness of sins as discussed in the study of Acts 2:38; its background is the washing or ritual cleansing ceremonies of the Old Testament. It is accomplished only by the application of the blood of Christ to our lives: "The blood of Jesus His Son cleanses us from all sin" (1 John 1:7). When Ananias says, "Get your sins washed away," he is simply saying, "Get your sins forgiven."

The significant point for our purposes is the close connection between baptism and the washing away of sins. The most natural understanding is that the former is somehow the occasion or the condition of the latter. This is true for several reasons. First, this is consistent with the situation as described in the last section. Saul is under deep conviction of his sins, and has been fasting and praying for three days while awaiting instruction as to what he should do about them. Thus when Ananias tells him to "be baptized and wash away your sins," the guilt-ridden Saul would most naturally take baptism to be what he should do to wash his sins away.

Second, this view is consistent with other New Testament teaching about baptism and salvation in general and with its teaching about baptism and forgiveness in particular. It is in effect the exact equivalent of Peter's instruction in Acts 2:38. "Be baptized for the forgiveness of your sins" means the very same thing as "be baptized and wash away your sins."

Third, the very fact that Saul is instructed with an *imperative* to *wash away his sins* shows that it must be the result of baptism. As noted above, the only true means of washing sins away is the blood of Christ. All would surely agree that only the Lord Himself can apply His blood to our souls. That is to say, the washing away of sins is an act of God and not the act of any human being. It is a spiritual act accomplished by divine power alone. It is impossible for Saul or anyone else literally to wash away his own

> Only the Lord Himself can apply His blood to our souls.

sins. What sense does it make, then, for Saul to be told to "wash away your sins"? How could he possibly do such a thing? Here is the answer: there was *no way* that he could do this himself *unless* the washing away of sins was dependent on something he *could* do, namely, submit to Christian baptism. This is the implication of the fact that "wash away" is in the imperative form.

Finally, the *number* and *order* of the imperatives show that baptism is a condition for washing away sins. If the outward act were *only* a symbolic picture of a prior inner cleansing, we would not expect him to put both in the imperative form. In such a case it would be appropriate for the "washing away" to be an aorist participle (like "rising up" and "calling upon"). Strictly speaking the action of an aorist participle *precedes* the action of the main verb. Ananias thus would have said, "Be baptized [imperative], having washed away your sins [aorist participle]." But he does not say this; he uses two imperatives instead.

But does the use of two imperatives in itself mean that baptism is a condition for washing away sins? Not necessarily. Both could be imperative, with baptism still being just a symbolic picture of the prior inner cleansing. But in this case, the imperatives would have to be reversed: "wash away your sins and be baptized." In fact, *only* if they were in this order could we say that baptism just pictures the prior cleansing. But they are not; "be baptized" — an imperative — precedes "wash away your sins" — an imperative. This order of the two imperatives, along with the other reasons cited above, requires us to conclude that baptism is a preceding condition for the washing away or forgiveness of sins.

The close connection between baptism and washing in Acts 22:16 helps us to understand the baptismal content of other New Testament references to washing. For example, Paul says to the converted sinners at Corinth, "But you were washed, but you were sanctified, but you were justified in the name of the Lord Jesus Christ, and in the Spirit of our God" (1 Cor. 6:11). All three verbs are in the aorist tense, referring to a single action in the past. The verb for "washed" is the same as that used in Acts 22:16, where the action is connected with baptism. This suggests that 1 Corinthians 6:11 is also referring to baptism.

The two modifying phrases in this verse in Corinthians also point to baptism. "In the name of the Lord Jesus Christ" recalls Matthew 28:19; Acts 2:38; 8:16; 10:48; 19:5; and 1 Corinthians 1:13. "In [en] the Spirit" is the same expression as Matthew 3:11 (and parallels); Acts 1:5; and Acts 11:16. These are all baptismal references. The fact that the two phrases are used to modify all three verbs shows that the latter are all referring to a single act, namely, baptism. "You were washed," at which time "you were sanctified" and "you were justified."

Another passage that speaks of washing is Hebrews 10:22, which says that we have had "our hearts sprinkled clean from an evil conscience and our bodies washed with pure water." That this speaks of baptism is clear not only from the reference to washing but also from its description as an application of water to our bodies. The statement as a whole refers to the inner and outer aspects of the "one baptism" (Eph. 4:5), namely, the cleansing of the heart from sin and the immersion of the body in water.

Two other inferences to washing that most probably are speaking of baptism are Ephesians 5:26 and Titus 3:5. These will be discussed in detail in separate chapters.

## Calling on His Name

Ananias instructs Saul to arise and be baptized, and wash away his sins, "calling on His name." The verb here is an aorist partici-

**71**

ple. This means that this action, while intimately connected with that of the main verbs, is nevertheless meant to precede it. Saul is thus told to "call on His name" as a preface to his baptism and the washing away of his sins.

What is the significance of this action? To understand this we must look to the origin of this expression in Joel and its use elsewhere in the New Testament, especially in Acts. The Old Testament source is Joel 2:32, "And it will come about that whoever calls on the name of the LORD will be delivered." Since this appears in connection with Joel's prophecy concerning the coming of the Spirit, we are not surprised that Peter quotes it in Acts 2:21, "And it shall be, that every one who calls on the name of the Lord shall be saved." Paul quotes it in Romans 10:13, "Whoever will call upon the name of the Lord will be saved." Christians are described as those who call upon His name (Acts 9:14,21; 1 Cor. 1:2).

> Christians are described as those who call upon His name.

Specifically, *whose* name is being called upon? In Joel it is the name of Yahweh ("Jehovah"), whom we know in the New Covenant revelation to include Father, Son, and Holy Spirit. In the New Testament passages the name "Lord" specifically refers to Jesus Christ. This is especially clear in Acts 9:13-17; Romans 10:9-13; and 1 Corinthians 1:2. Thus, although no specific name is mentioned in Acts 22:16, it undoubtedly refers to calling on the name of the Lord Jesus Christ.

Now the crucial question is this: *for what purpose* or *to what end* was Saul told to call upon the name of the Lord? Here again the answer is not in doubt. He must call upon the name of the Lord *for salvation*. This is Joel's point: "Whoever calls on the name of the LORD *will be delivered*." This is how Peter and Paul quote it: whoever calls on the name of the Lord *will be saved*. Paul equates it with the confession of the mouth that Jesus is Lord, a confession that results in salvation (Rom. 10:9-10; cf. 10:13).

Thus Ananias's instruction does no less than confirm the unanimous Biblical testimony to the saving significance of baptism. God has promised to save us — to give us forgiveness of sins and the gift of the Holy Spirit — in Christian baptism. As a person prepares to be baptized, he should call upon God to keep this promise; he should call upon the Lord Jesus Christ to apply His cleansing blood to his sinful heart and to send the gift of the Holy Spirit. It is a prayer of faith in the faithfulness of God.

As it applied to Saul it meant two things. First, the fact that he was supposed to call upon the Lord's name in connection with his baptism meant that he had not yet received salvation. The whole point of his calling upon the Lord's name was *to be saved*. Thus this is one final confirmation of the conclusion already reached above, that Saul was not saved on the Damascus Road nor during his three days of fasting and prayer. He was not saved until he called upon the Lord's name in baptism. Second, this "calling upon His name" was an indication of Saul's *faith* in Jesus. We may note that there is no specific mention of faith in Ananias's instruction, but it is implied nevertheless. According to Romans 10:14, one cannot call upon Him unless he has believed in Him. Thus Saul is here being told to do what every good Jew has to do now that the Messiah has come, namely, transform his limited Old Covenant faith into the fully rounded faith that accepts Jesus as Jahweh Himself and as the source of salvation.

## Summary

In this chapter we have explored the teaching of Acts 22:16 on the meaning of baptism. First we recounted the basic facts of Saul's encounters with Jesus and Ananias, and concluded that he was not yet saved when Ananias instructed him concerning baptism. We noted that Ananias gave him the gospel offer of the double cure: forgiveness (the "washing away" of the guilt of his sins) and the Holy Spirit.

Next, we concentrated on the relation between baptism and the washing away of sins. We concluded that the only reasonable understanding of Ananias's words is that the washing takes place in the act of baptism. This is consistent with the context and with other New Testament teaching. Also, it is required by the fact that "wash away" is an imperative as such, and also by the number and order of the two imperatives in the verse.

Finally we saw that "calling on His name" refers to calling on the name of Jesus for His promised salvation. That this precedes baptism is shown by the participial construction and confirms the fact that baptism is for salvation. The sinner approaches baptism calling upon the Lord to save him as He has promised.

> "Calling on His name" refers to calling on the name of Jesus for His promised salvation.

## NOTES

1. In his brief retelling of this event to King Agrippa, Paul does not mention the role of Ananias. His summary of his commission in 26:16-18 is most likely what Jesus told him later through Ananias, rather than something spoken directly to him on the Damascus road.

2. Hans von Soden, "ἀδελφός, etc.," *Theological Dictionary of the New Testament,* ed. Gerhard Kittel, tr. Geoffrey W. Bromiley (Grand Rapids: Eerdmans, 1964), 1:145.

3. Acts 2:29,37; 3:17; 7:2,23; 13:15,26,38; 22:1,5; 23:1,5-6; 28:17,21. See also Luke 6:42 and Heb. 7:5.

# ~7~
# ROMANS 6:3-4

Thus far we have considered three passages in the Gospels and two in the book of Acts that tell us something about the meaning of baptism. All of these passages are anticipatory of baptism, that is, they are statements and exhortations recorded prior to baptism itself. The statements in the Gospels were made by Jesus before Christian baptism had even been instituted. The exhortations in Acts were part of the gospel offer made to sinners, inviting them to receive salvation.

The rest of the passages to be considered in this book are taken from the epistles, and they all deal with baptism as an accomplished fact. They are statements made primarily to Christians who have already been baptized. They are meant to increase our understanding of the meaning of our own baptism. They tell us more about what actually happened when we were baptized.

The first of these passages is Romans 6:3-4, which says, "Or do you not know that all of us who have been baptized into Christ Jesus have been baptized into His death? Therefore we have been buried with Him through baptism into death, in order that as Christ was raised from the dead through the glory of the Father, so we too might walk in newness of life." What is the Apostle Paul telling us here about the meaning of our baptism?

## Union with Christ

The basic point of the passage is that we are "baptized into Christ Jesus," namely, into a saving union with Christ our Redeemer. The concept of union with Christ occurs quite frequently in Scripture. It is a comprehensive description of the saved state. All other aspects of salvation come to us as the result of our being united with Christ.

The terminology expressing this union varies, but the main terms are that we are in Christ and Christ is in us. Regarding the former, for example, Paul refers to "all the saints *in Christ Jesus*" at Philippi (Phil. 1:1; see Col. 1:2); and Peter declares, "Peace be to you all who are *in Christ*" (1 Pet. 5:14). "By His doing you are *in Christ Jesus*," says Paul (1 Cor. 1:30). Regarding the other expression, Paul says that as Christians you should know "that Jesus Christ is *in you*" (2 Cor. 13:5). "If Christ is *in you*," he says, your spirit is alive (Rom. 8:10). "Christ *in you*" is "the hope of glory" (Col. 1:27). Thus he prays "that Christ may *dwell in your hearts*" (Eph. 3:17). "It is no longer I who live, but Christ *lives in me*," is his testimony of himself (Gal. 2:20).

What does it mean to say that we have a union with Christ, such that both He is in us and we are in Him? These statements are not meant to describe physical location, but the closeness of our relationship to our Savior. The specific point is that our relationship with Christ is so close that all the power and life that spring from His redeeming work belong to us and flow into our lives. All the redemptive benefits of His death, burial, and resurrection are ours. Thus Paul says that we are united with Him specifically in His death and in His resurrection (Rom. 6:5).

What are the results of our being united with Christ in his death and resurrection? What specific benefits are ours through this union? No less than the double cure. Since Jesus died for the express purpose of taking our guilt upon Himself and paying the eternal penalty for our sins, when we are united with Him in his death our guilt is removed and our status before God is such that our penalty is considered paid. The blood that He shed in His death is applied to our guilty souls and becomes our shield to protect us from the deserved wrath of God. Thus because of this union with Christ we are forgiven or justified. As Romans 8:1

says, "There is therefore now no condemnation for those who are *in Christ Jesus.*"

But there is more. Our union with Christ also provides us with the other part of the double cure, namely, our regeneration or rebirth to new life. This is the main point here in Romans 6. Being united with Christ in *His* death, burial, and resurrection means that we experience a death, burial, and resurrection of our own. Just as Christ died with reference to the sins of the whole world, in our union with Him we die to our own sin (Rom. 6:10-11). Our old sin-prone self actually experiences a death (Rom. 6:6) and is buried out of sight just as Jesus was (Rom. 6:4). Then, just as Jesus arose from the dead, in our union with Him we too experience an actual resurrection from spiritual death and begin to live a new life (Rom. 6:4-5; cf. Eph. 2:1,5-6). This is the same ideas as 2 Corinthians 5:17, "Therefore if any man is *in Christ,* he is a new creature; the old things passed away; behold, new things have come." We can see, then, how crucially important our union with Christ is. It is the key to our salvation. Embodied in this one reality are our freedom from both the guilt and the power of sin.

> Just as Jesus arose from the dead, in our union with Him we too experience an actual resurrection from spiritual death.

## Baptized into Christ

In view of this importance we should be vitally interested in the time when this union with Christ begins. Exactly when does our death to sin occur, and exactly when do we receive "newness of life"? How does Romans 6 answer this question?

Though the text seems to be clear and unequivocal on this point, it is a matter of serious disagreement. At least three answers have been given. One is that our death and resurrection with Christ took place on the historical occasion of His own death and resurrection, over nineteen centuries ago. The idea here is that we were actually in Christ or were a part of Christ when He went to the cross, so we were literally "crucified with Him" (see Romans 6:6). When He came forth from the tomb, we were actually in Him and thus arose with Him. This view is most popular among those who hold to the view of limited atonement (such as Calvinists). They say that *only the elect* were in Christ on the cross and at the tomb; hence His saving work applies only to the elect. Also, their presence in Christ at that time *guarantees* their salvation.

(This last point is well taken. If this is the correct view, then whoever was "in Christ" at the time of His saving work will surely be saved, since that person has already literally suffered the penalty for his sins. Thus the only ones who can consistently hold this view are Calvinists and Universalists. If only the elect were in Christ on the cross and at the tomb, then only the elect will be saved. But if the whole race was in Christ there, then the whole race will be saved.)

Those who hold this first view characteristically have a weak view of baptism. They either deny that Romans 6 is speaking of *water* baptism at all,[1] or say that baptism is only *symbolizing* the death and resurrection we experienced with Christ when He died and rose again nearly two thousand years ago.

A second view as to the time of our death to sin and resurrection to new life is that this happens as soon as the heart turns to God in faith and/or repentance. This is probably the most common view. It is very popular in Protestantism in general, being held by many of those who have a "faith only" concept of salvation (especially if they do not hold the first view above). It is the view expressed in the popular contemporary song, "Water Grave," whose words include something like this: "I'm goin' down to the river; I'm gonna be buried alive; I'm gonna show my heavenly Father that the man I used to be finally died." This means that the death and resurrection have already occurred prior to baptism, which is a subsequent symbolic demonstration of that fact.

This second view is also quite prevalent in literature of the Restoration Movement, past and present. The death and resurrection are commonly said to be the result of repentance. When a person repents, he puts his old life behind him (this is the death) and determines to live for God (this is the new life). Thus the death and resurrection have already been accomplished before baptism, which again only symbolizes these realities. After all (it is commonly said), we do not bury something unless it is already dead, do we?

Both of these first two views seem to stumble over the text itself, however, which presents a third view. In a very clear and straightforward manner. Romans 6:3-4 affirms that *baptism* is the time when we are united with Christ in His death and resurrection, and thus the time when we experience our own death to sin and resurrection to new life.

> **Baptism is the time when we are united with Christ in His death and resurrection.**

In general terms verse three reminds us that we have been "baptized into Christ Jesus." The word *into* is again the Greek word *eis,* which has been discussed at some length in connection with Acts 2:38. In its basic meaning this preposition indicates *motion toward* a destination or goal, especially when used with an action verb. The verb *baptized* is certainly an action verb, with the destination or goal being Christ Jesus Himself. Thus to be "baptized into" Christ means that baptism is the action that moves us or carries us "into Christ," viz., into that close relationship with Him that makes us partakers of the benefits of His saving work.

This is essentially the same as being baptized "into [*eis*] the name of" the Father, Son, and Spirit, as discussed earlier in reference to Matthew 28:19. Both expressions ("baptized into Christ" and "baptized into the name of Christ") speak of entering into an intimate relationship with our Lord in Christian baptism. See also Galatians 3:27 for the same idea. (This passage will be treated in detail in a later chapter.)

In Romans 6:3-4 Paul assumes that every Christian already knows that he has been baptized into Christ. His point here is to show us specifically what this means. Don't you know, he says, "that all of us who have been baptized into Christ Jesus have been *baptized into His death*"? In the context he reminds us that Jesus died for our sins not only in the sense that He paid their penalty, but also in that He died to defeat sin and destroy its power and

**79**

do away with it (see 6:6-10). And every Christian has come within the scope of this sin-destroying force of the death of Christ; we have tapped into its lethal power. When did we do this? In our baptism. There is absolutely no indication that this union with Christ in His death happened as soon as we believed or repented. We did not believe into His death; we did not repent into His death. Paul explicitly says we "have been baptized into His death" (v. 3). If this is not plain enough, he repeats the idea in verse 4: "We have been buried with Him *through baptism* into death." Those who say that our union with Christ in His death, and thus our own death to sin, occurred before baptism are simply not taking the text at its word.[2]

What is true of our union with Christ in His death is true also of our union with Him in His resurrection. This passage does not speak explicitly of our being baptized into Christ's resurrection or being raised up with Christ in baptism, but the implication is quite clear. The logical and chronological connection between death and resurrection is such that union with Christ in resurrection could certainly not occur prior to union with Him in death. Verse 4 specifically says that we were buried with Him through baptism into death for the very purpose of experiencing resurrection with Him, too. "For if we have become united with Him in the likeness of His death, certainly we shall be also in the likeness of His resurrection" (v. 5). Colossians 2:12 does explicitly say that our resurrection with Christ occurs in baptism. (This passage will be discussed fully in a later chapter.)

Paul is telling us, then, that the historical events of the saving work of Jesus have their counterpart or fulfillment in a specific historical event in the life of every Christian, namely, our baptism. Christ's crucifixion and resurrection are the events which save us, but the power of these saving acts is applied to us in baptism. As Oepke says, "Baptism . . . is for individuals the actualisation of this relation to salvation history."[3] Just as Christ really died and rose again, in our baptism we too really died and rose again in a spiritual sense by virtue of our being brought into a relationship with His death and resurrection at that point.

It would certainly not be out of place to comment at this point on the propriety of immersion as the only valid form of baptism. The reference to baptism as a *burial* with Christ (v. 4; see Col. 2:12) in itself underscores this fact. But the concept of burial should not be emphasized in isolation from the aspects of death and resurrection. In fact, the dying and rising with Christ are the main elements of baptism; burial is in a sense only incidental to these. Or rather, the main point is the full and unbroken sequence of death, burial, and resur-

> The dying and rising with Christ are the main elements of baptism.

rection, all of which are represented by the single act of baptism. It cannot be disputed that immersion is the only form of baptism that pictures this whole sequence; no other form even comes close. This connection must be intentional; God appointed immersion for this purpose because of its unique ability visually to represent death, burial and resurrection — both Christ's and our own.

This acknowledges that baptism *is* a symbolic representation of a deeper reality, an "outward sign of an inward grace," as the common description goes. This is a truth denied by practically no one. The serious error often connected with this truth, however, is that baptism symbolizes a reality that has *already occurred*. This would be true if we were thinking only of the death, burial, and resurrection *of Jesus;* in this case it does symbolize a past reality. But this is not true with regard to ourselves. In our case Scripture consistently teaches that baptism as the external symbol occurs *simultaneously* with the spiritual reality it is symbolizing. In Romans 6 that reality is the death and burial of our old life of sin and our resurrection to new life. It is a reality that occurs because we are "baptized into Christ."

## The Basis for Holy Living

Paul affirms in Romans 6:3-4 that our union with Christ begins in baptism, resulting in our personal death to sin and resurrection to a new life in Christ. This is equivalent to the new birth of John 3:5, which is related to baptism and to the Spirit. It is also the same purpose for which the Spirit is promised in Acts 2:38-39, viz., inner regeneration. These are all just different ways of referring to the same reality: being born again, being regenerated, dying to sin and rising again with Christ. This is accomplished within our soul specifically by the Holy Spirit, whose presence within us as a gift is one of the main benefits of the redemptive work of Christ and our union with Him.

What is the significance of this Spirit-wrought resurrection within our souls? Basically it is a change within us that breaks the grip of sin upon our hearts and makes it possible for us to live a life that is holy and pleasing to God. The reality of this change is the main point of the context of Romans 6:3-4.

> Basically it is a change within us that breaks the grip of sin upon our hearts.

In the first five chapters of Romans Paul has established the fact that we are justified by faith in Christ's saving work rather than by our own works done in obedience to God's law. Such is the essence of salvation by grace. In chapters 6 and 7 he is dealing with possible objections that might be raised in opposition to this teaching. The first is that such an idea would seem to encourage people to sin all the more. "What shall we say then? Are we to continue in sin that grace might increase?" (Rom. 6:1). In response to this objection Paul appeals to the event of our baptism and to the reality of the regeneration that has occurred there.

In effect Paul is saying that anyone who thinks grace gives him a license to go on sinning after he has been saved just doesn't understand it is a *double* cure. Being saved is more than being justified or having forgiveness for sins. It also involves that change in our souls that makes holy living natural for us and sin a contradiction to our basic nature. Here he speaks in terms of death and resurrection. He cries, "How shall we who died to sin still live in it?" (Rom. 6:2).

Someone might respond, "What do you mean, Paul, that we have 'died to sin'?" Then comes Paul's didactic questioning, to this effect: "What? You mean you don't know what happened to you when you were baptized? You don't know that when you were baptized into Christ, you were baptized into His very death? And just as surely as His death was followed by His resurrection, don't you know that you too were raised up to walk in newness of life?" (Rom. 6:3-4). Because of this personal inner death and resurrection, we as Christians no longer have any excuse for sin or any reason to sin. Sin's grip on our hearts is broken; we are free from its enslaving power (Rom. 6:6-7). Holiness is no longer just a duty to be slavishly pursued, but a blessed possibility to be grasped with joy and thanksgiving. Such is the nature of our salvation.

What a beautiful and welcome lesson this is for any serious and sincere Christian! How comforting to know that we have within ourselves the basis for holy living, that we have been "created in Christ Jesus for good works" (Eph. 2:10)! But when did this happen to us? When did we experience this wonderful reality? In your baptism, says Paul. And how can we keep the reality of our newness of life in our minds? By remembering your baptism! Don't forget what God did for you in your baptism! What Christian has not lamented, "If only I could die to my sin!" The liberating truth is that *we already have* — in baptism! As Christians who have been baptized into Christ's death, it is our privilege to build upon the reality bestowed therein, through the power of the Spirit who continues to indwell us.

> How comforting to know that we have within ourselves the basis for holy living.

Here is a fact that cannot be avoided. When Paul wants to emphasize the unthinkableness of sin and the possibility and expectation of holy living in the Christian's life, he appeals to what happened in our baptism. He does not say, "Remember when you first believed" or "Don't you know what happened when you first repented"; he does not say, "Think about the time you bowed your head and received Christ into your heart." He says, "Remember your baptism!" Why should he so magnify baptism if this were not the specific point where the life-changing and heart-renewing work of God was actually accomplished?

**83**

# Summary

In this chapter we have seen that Romans 6:3-4 deals with the basic reality of our union with Christ, specifically our union with Him in His saving death and resurrection. The result is not only forgiveness of sins but also our own death to sin and resurrection to new life. The latter is the focal point of this context.

We have also seen that, according to this text, our union with Christ and thus our spiritual death and resurrection (another way of describing regeneration) occurred in our baptism. Other views as to the time of our dying and rising again cannot do justice to the clear affirmation that we are buried with Him *through baptism* into death. The centrality of death, burial, and resurrection in the symbolism of baptism shows the appropriateness of immersion as its only mode.

Finally we have seen that the spiritual works wrought within our hearts at baptism are the divinely-given basis for holy living. Thus grace does not open the door to more and more sin. It does just the opposite: it closes the door on sin and shuts it out of our lives, if only we will live up to the potential bestowed upon us in our baptism.

## NOTES

1. One of my professors at Westminster Theological Seminary (Jay Adams) exclaimed in class one day, "There's not a drop of water in Romans 6!"
2. The idea that baptism as a *burial* implies that death has already occured is an inference that goes contrary to the text itself. Romans 6:4 does not say we are buried in baptism because we have *already* died; it says we are buried through baptism *into* death.
3. Albrecht Oepke, "λούω, etc.," *Theological Dictionary of the New Testament,* ed. Gerhard Kittel, tr. Geoffrey W. Bromiley (Grand Rapids: Eerdmans, 1967), IV:303.

# ≈ 8 ≈

# 1 CORINTHIANS 12:13

The next passage dealing with the meaning of baptism is 1 Corinthians 12:13, which says, "For by one Spirit we were all baptized into one body, whether Jews or Greeks, whether slaves or free, and we were all made to drink of one Spirit." This deals with one theme that should be familiar by now, namely, the relation between baptism and the Holy Spirit. Two other concepts appear here for the first time, though: baptism and church membership, and baptism and unity.

## Baptized in the Spirit

We have already discussed the Holy Spirit and baptism in some detail, especially in relation to Acts 2:38; but we have not yet examined the meaning of the expression "baptized in the Spirit." Though it is not immediately obvious because of the word order, this expression is used here in 1 Corinthians 12:13. We have all been baptized in the Spirit, says Paul.

This expression occurs in six other verses in the New Testament.[1] Four of these are in the Gospels and are just parallel reports of John's announcement of the Messiah, "I baptized you with water; but He will baptize you with the Holy Spirit" (Mark 1:8; see Matt. 3:11; Luke 3:16; John 1:33). The other two are in the book of Acts and are simply repetitive of this original statement by John (Acts 1:5; 11:16). As a general pattern the verb *baptize* is followed by the prepositional phrase *in the Holy Spirit*, in which "in" translates the Greek word *en*. In one case (Acts 1:5) the verb is in the middle of

**85**

the phrase, but this has no bearing on the meaning or emphasis. In one case (Mark 1:8) the preposition is omitted in some manuscripts, but the dative case yields the same meaning.

Except for differences that have to do with emphasis, the expression as it occurs in 1 Corinthians 12:13 is the same as in these other six verses. Because the emphasis here is on unity, the prepositional phrase is given first and precedes the verb; and it reads "in *one* Spirit" rather than "in the *Holy* Spirit." But the principal words and meanings are exactly the same as in the other six verses: the verb is the same *(baptize);* the preposition is the same *(en);* the Spirit is the same.

There is some disagreement over the translation of the preposition *en*. The word can mean "in" or "with," in the sense that the Spirit is the *element in which* we are baptized; or it can mean "by," in the sense that the Spirit is the *agent by which* we are baptized. In John's original statement the former is the preferred meaning, since there baptism *in* or *with* the Spirit is compared to baptism in water and fire (Matt. 3:11; Luke 3:16), and the latter are elements rather than agents; and since the Messiah is specified as the agent who does the baptizing. In the context of 1 Corinthians 12:13, however, the same expression *("en* the Spirit")  is used in the other sense (vv. 3,9) where the Spirit is the agent performing a certain activity. Thus there are reasons for taking it both ways in verse 13. Beasley-Murray is right, though, when he says, "Basically the meaning is not greatly affected" either way.[2] Possibly both ideas are included: the Spirit as agent baptizes us in Himself as element. We will continue to speak of "baptized in the Spirit."

What does it mean to be "baptized in the Spirit"? This concept, with related expressions such as "Holy Spirit baptism" and "Spirit-baptized," is understood in several different ways in modern Christendom. In Reformation-oriented church groups (e.g., Presbyterian, Reformed, Baptist) it most commonly refers to the moment when the sinner is born again through God's initial bestowing of the Spirit for the purpose of salvation. This Spirit baptism is simultaneous with the

**What does it mean to be "baptized in the Spirit"?**

beginning of faith, either as its cause (for Calvinists) or as its result (for non-Calvinists). It is completely distinct from baptism in water. Spirit baptism (and thus salvation) comes first, to be followed at a later time by water baptism.[3]

In many Wesleyan-oriented church groups (especially holiness and Pentecostal) and in charismatic circles, "baptized in the Spirit" is given a quite different meaning. Here it refers to an event that takes place after conversion and after water baptism, an event in which the Holy Spirit baptizes the Christian with a fresh outpouring of grace. For some this is believed to result in fullness of sanctification; for others it is the bestowal of miraculous powers, especially the power to speak in tongues. In itself it is not a saving act, though some take it (especially the tongues) to be a necessary *sign* that the person is saved. Except for those who take this latter view, Spirit baptism is something that all Christians *may* experience but which in fact some do not.

Within the Restoration Movement still a third view of "baptized in the Spirit" is quite popular. This view is similar to the previous one in that it sees Spirit baptism as the special bestowal of miraculous powers, especially speaking in tongues, and not as a saving act. But here the similarity ends. According to this view, only two instances of Spirit baptism have ever occurred, viz., Pentecost (Acts 2) and the household of Cornelius (Acts 10). It was never intended for anyone else. And in these two cases, it occurred prior to water baptism, not after it.

The one thing all of these views have in common is that baptism in the Spirit is distinct from baptism in water. For some it comes before it, and for some it comes afterwards; but in all cases it is separated from water baptism by an interval of time, sometimes quite lengthy.

In my opinion none of the above views is correct. In my best understanding Holy Spirit baptism is something every Christian has experienced: "By one Spirit we were *all* baptized," says Paul. Also, its purpose is to bestow salvation, not miraculous powers. As we have seen in our study of Acts 2:38, the miraculous manifestations at Pentecost and at Cornelius's conversion were unique exceptions and were not meant to be part of the essence of normal Spirit baptism. Its essence is rather the saving work of the Spirit in which He regenerates the sinner and begins to indwell him; in short, it is the second part of the double cure described earlier. Finally, Spirit baptism occurs simultaneously with water baptism, or more accu-

> **Spirit baptism occurs simultaneously with water baptism.**

rately, it is the inner aspect of our one baptism. In accord with what we have already seen in connection with John 3:5 and Acts 2:38, this saving work of the Spirit (viz., baptism in the Spirit) is something that happened to all of us when we were baptized in water.

The separation of Spirit baptism and water baptism into two distinct events is one of the most serious and far-reaching doctrinal errors ever introduced into Christendom.[4] To say that there are two separate baptisms in normal Christian experience contradicts the specific teaching of Ephesians 4:5, "One Lord, one faith, *one baptism*." Though it has two aspects, an outward and an inward, baptism is but a single event. Our one Lord has two natures, the divine and the human. Our one faith has two aspects, assent and trust. And our one baptism has two sides, water and Spirit. When a Christian looks back to the time of his conversion, he does not distinguish two separate points each known as baptism. When we find a reference to baptism in the Bible, we do not have to ask ourselves to which it refers — our Spirit baptism or our water baptism. There is only *one* baptism to which it *can* refer, namely, the only baptism any of us has experienced: that single moment when our bodies were immersed in water and our spirits immersed in the Holy Spirit.

That the Spirit acts in a saving way in baptism is clearly taught in passages such as John 3:5, Acts 2:38, and Titus 3:5. That His saving work should itself be called *baptism* is thus appropriate, but in a sense is quite incidental. From the standpoint of the pre-Pentecostal promises, the important point was that the Messiah would come and would *give* us the Holy Spirit as a regenerating, indwelling presence. Whether this bestowing of the Spirit is called baptism or something else is not the main point. The terminology in fact is derived from the circumstances in which John made his original promise. His main point was to call attention to the vast difference between himself and the coming Messiah. One distinction was that the latter would bring the long-awaited gift of the Holy Spirit. He couched the distinction in terms that were suggested by the immediate surroundings — his baptizing work. I only baptize you in water, he said; but the Messiah will "baptize" you in the Spirit. This particular term is incidental; the concept could be worded in different ways.

Jesus Himself put the same promise in different terms. He spoke to the woman at the well about *drinking* the gift of *living water* (John 4:10,14). This particular language is likewise suggested by the immediate surroundings. The same imagery is used in John 7:37-38, as Jesus cried out, saying, "If any man is thirsty, let him come to Me and drink. He who believes in Me, as the Scripture said, 'From his innermost being shall flow rivers of living water.'" It is commonly agreed that Jesus' language about drinking living water is an allusion to a ceremony prominent in that particular feast (v. 37), one which involved a pitcher of water. It is most instructive, then, when the Apostle John specifically equates the "living water" with the Spirit who would be given after Jesus' glorification in heaven (v. 39). Thus these references to *drinking* living water (the Spirit) are just another way of talking about how we receive the gift of the Holy Spirit. Whether we call it "being baptized in the Spirit" or "drinking the Spirit" is incidental.

In fact, 1 Corinthians 12:13 includes *both* of these figurative ways of speaking; it refers back to both of these incidents in the Gospels and their common promise of the Spirit. "By one Spirit we were all *baptized* into one body," it says, using the Baptist's term; "we were all made to *drink* of one Spirit," it says, using Jesus' term. Both refer to the same event, namely, when Jesus gave us the gift of the Holy Spirit in Christian baptism.

When the Corinthian Christians first read this statement, that "by one Spirit we were all baptized into one body," the references to baptism would have triggered only one memory in their minds, namely, the time they were immersed in water in order to receive the gift of the Holy Spirit. This is what it should mean to us, too.

# Baptism and the Church

Another main element in this verse is the relation between baptism and membership in the church of Jesus Christ. By the one Spirit we were all baptized "into [*eis*] one body," it says. From this we learn that baptism is the point or mode of entry into the church.

The "one body" is the one *church* of our Lord. Paul frequently compares the church with the human body,[5] especially to emphasize the headship of Christ and the unity of God's people. The latter is the main point of this context (1 Cor. 12:12-30), as will be seen in the next point ("Baptism and Unity") below. Regarding verse 13 we simply need to note that entry into the "one body" is the same as entry into the one church.

Paul says specifically that we are *baptized into* the church. The word *into* again is the Greek word *eis,* indicating motion toward a goal. The goal is membership in Christ's church, and baptism is the action that moves us to that goal. Such a statement should not surprise us in view of what we have already seen in connection with Romans 6:3-4, which says that we are "baptized into [*eis*] Christ Jesus." If we have been baptized into Christ, it makes sense that we have been baptized into His body. This also corresponds to John 3:3-5, where being "born of water" is a condition for entering the kingdom of God.

Some may be surprised to learn that almost everyone in Christendom agrees that there is a connection between baptism and church membership. A crucial point here, however, is the distinction between the *visible* church and the *invisible* church. Is this distinction valid? Many in the Restoration Movement deny it.

> Almost everyone in Christendom agrees that there is a connection between baptism and church membership.

They deny the existence of such a thing as an "invisible" church and often speak of it as one of the more diabolical human inventions.

I must insist, however, that such a distinction is quite Scripturally valid, at least in one important sense. I agree with the important Restoration premise that the New Testament gives us (at least in general outline) a discernible pattern for the church in terms of organization and polity. Once this pattern is discerned, we can visibly distinguish between a church that is following it and one which is not. One of our main goals is to make the "visible church" conform to this pattern.

At the same time, very few would insist that the membership lists of all the congregations that follow the New Testament pattern are the exact equivalent of the list of all Christians in the world today. (By "Christians" I mean those who are actually saved, those who have received the "double cure" of salvation through Christ.) Another important Restoration premise is that there are Christians among the sects or denominations, namely, among those church groups whose visible structure does not conform to the New Testament pattern. On the other hand, it should be obvious that some of those whose names are on the membership rolls of New Testament congregations are hypocrites and apostates (see Matt. 13:47-50). But what human being is able to discern which of those outside the New Testament-sanctioned (visible) churches are truly saved, and which of those within them are really not? Not a single one of us. Only God can see the hearts of men; only God has infallible knowledge of who is really "in Christ" or in the body of Christ.

This is the sense in which there is an *invisible* church. The border that separates the saved from the unsaved is visible only to God and invisible to us finite human beings. Everyone who is saved is truly a member of the body of which Christ is head and Savior (Eph. 5:23), a member of the church which Christ loved and for which He gave Himself up (Eph. 5:25). This is the one universal church whose borders are invisible to us. Now, since the New Testament does reveal the ideal polity or organization within which God wants His people to live and to serve Him, we must say that many of those who may be members of the invisible church are not being obedient to God's will as long as they remain members of unbiblical denominational organizations or of no church at all. But this is a question of incomplete sanctification; it does not negate their salvation as long as it is not a deliberate defiance of the Lordship of Christ. Thus they remain in the invisible church though they are not members of a biblically-sanctioned visible church congregation.[6]

For example, a person may be converted in a Methodist or Catholic context yet insist on being immersed into Christ for the forgiveness of sins and the gift of the Holy Spirit. Or a teenager may be converted at Christian camp and be immersed into Christ before formally becoming a member of a particular local congregation. Such persons are surely within the "one body" that is under the blood of Christ.

We should note that the "one body" to which 1 Corinthians 12:13 refers corresponds to the *invisible* church. This is generally the case with all references to the church as the body of Christ, e.g., "He is also head of the body, the church" (Col. 1:18). The reference to *one* body (see Eph. 4:4) even more clearly shows that the one universal church is in view rather than a single local congregation.

Now, all of this relates to the question of baptism and church membership in a very important way. The common Protestant (faith-only) view is that baptism is the means of entry into the *visible* church (as they understand it), but that it has no particular connection with membership in the *invisible* church. To be more specific, *Holy Spirit* baptism, as a separate event from water baptism, is the point at which one enters the invisible church (and thus is saved), while *water* baptism is the point of entry into some visible church.

But as we have already seen, the Bible does not separate Holy Spirit baptism from water baptism; there is only *one baptism*. When Scripture speaks of our being baptized, it is referring to water baptism during which the Spirit is working. Thus when 1 Corinthians 12:13 says that we are "baptized into one body," it means that *water* baptism is the time when we enter the *invisible* church of Jesus Christ, whether we at that time become members of a visible church or not. We cannot stress strongly enough that the Biblical view is thus the very opposite of the view commonly taught in Protestantism. The New Testament *never* depicts baptism as simply a public act by which one enters some visible, local congregation. It is always a matter of salvation and thus entry into the invisible, universal church that is the body of Christ. A good example of this is the Ethiopian eunuch, whose baptism occurred in a wilderness area and was in no way even remotely connected with his membership in a local congregation (Acts 8:26-39).

> **Water baptism is the time when we enter the invisible church of Jesus Christ.**

Thus to be baptized into the one body of Christ means that whoever receives Biblical baptism with a believing, repentant heart is a part of the church for which Jesus died, whatever visible church group he or she belongs to at the time, if any.

## Baptism and Unity

The main emphasis in 1 Corinthians 12 is the *unity* of all Christians. There is but *one* body. This remains true even when our own weaknesses and foibles tend to divide Christians from one another and fragment the body of Christ on a visible level. This seems to have been a particularly serious problem at Corinth. One cause of division was the arbitrary categorizing of spiritual gifts into the more and the less important or prestigious kinds. It is in this context that Paul reminds them and us that there is only one body, and we all came into it in the same way, namely: by one Spirit we were all baptized into that body.

The ultimate basis of the church's unity is the one God Himself, in terms of the one Spirit, the one Lord (Paul's usual name for Jesus or God the Son), and the one God (Paul's usual term for God the Father), as 1 Corinthians 12:4-6 indicates.[7] The

**The main emphasis in 1 Corinthians 12 is the unity of all Christians.** main emphasis is on the one Spirit, who is the one immediate source of the spiritual gifts bestowed upon the church (1 Cor. 12:7-11). Even though church members possess a manifold variety of gifts, we are what we are not because of some greater or less accomplishment of our own, but because of the common action of the same Spirit upon us all.

But even more basic to our unity than the common origin of our gifts is the common origin of our very membership in the church. That is, the church (body) is one because we all — every member of it — came into it by the same doorway: the one Holy Spirit's action in the *one baptism.* Thus baptism itself is one basis of the unity of all Christians. Those who have received the same baptism are a part of the same body. This agrees with Ephesians 4:5, where the "one baptism" is in the list of unifying factors of the church. It also agrees with Galatians 3:27-28, which says that all who have been baptized into Christ are one in Him.

One of the main goals of the Restoration Movement has always been to bring all those who have received this common baptism by the same Spirit into one *visible* body where their unity is not only real but also openly manifested before the whole world. This one visible body can be no less than the church whose pattern is revealed in the apostles' teaching. This is the essence of the "Restoration plea."

## Summary

First Corinthians 12:13 teaches first of all that all Christians have been "baptized in the Spirit." It is wrong to separate this Spirit baptism from water baptism, or to link it exclusively with miraculous gifts, or to limit it to Pentecost and Cornelius. Spirit baptism is part of the same event as water baptism; its purpose is salvation; and it has been experienced by all Christians. There is only ONE baptism. Whenever we read in Scripture about our "baptism," we do not have to try to decide whether it means

Spirit baptism or water baptism, as if these were two separate events. There is only one baptism, when we were immersed in water for the gift of the Spirit.

The second thing taught in this passage is that baptism is the doorway into the church; we were all "baptized into one body." The one body is the church; we came into it or became members of it by means of baptism. Although many say that this refers only to membership in the visible or local church, this is not the case. Baptism is when we come into the "one body" of Christ, which is sometimes called the invisible church, the group of people who are under the saving blood of Christ.

The final point of this passage is that baptism is one important basis for the *unity* of the church. What makes the body *one* is its relation to the one God, especially the working of the one Holy Spirit at the time of our one baptism. Thus the church is one because we all entered the one body in the same way, through the one baptism.

## NOTES

1. Another passage with a parallel expression is 1 Corinthians 6:11, where the word *washed* is used instead of *baptized*. We have all been "washed in [*en*] the Spirit," it says.

2. Beasley-Murray, *Baptism in the New Testament*, 167.

3. This would be the uniform pattern for adults. In the case of infants (for those who believe in infant baptism), water baptism may precede Spirit baptism by many years.

4. John's statement, "I baptized you with water; but He will baptize you with the Holy Spirit," reflects only a distinction between John's baptism, which was with water *only*, and Christian baptism, which is with water *and* Spirit.

5. Rom. 12:4-5; 1 Cor. 10:17; 12:12-30; Eph. 1:22-23; 3:6; 4:4,12-16; 5:23,30; Col. 1:18,24; 2:19; 3:15.

6. We should note that God cares about *both* the visible and invisible church. Just because the latter is the one in which membership is indispensable for salvation does not mean that membership in the former is a matter of indifference to God. One cannot be completely pleasing to God until he is a member both of the invisible body of the saved *and* the divinely ordained visible church. This is one of the indispensable presuppositions of the Restoration Movement.

7. This parallels the point made in Ephesians 4:3-6.

# ~9~
# GALATIANS 3:26-27

The next passage with information on the meaning of baptism is Galatians 3:26-27, which reads, "For you are all sons of God through faith in Christ Jesus. For all of you who were baptized into Christ have clothed yourselves with Christ." The key to understanding this passage is the concept of sonship as related to heirship. This is summarized in Galatians 4:7, "Therefore you are no longer a slave, but a son; and if a son, then an heir through God."

The main point for our purposes will be this: the state of *sonship*, which qualifies us to inherit God's blessings of salvation, is entered into in Christian baptism.[1]

## Sons of God

To understand the point of Galatians 3:26-27, we must understand the point of the whole Context of Galatians 3:1–4:7. The central idea here is the significance of Abraham and our role as *sons* of Abraham. According to Paul the gospel itself was preached to Abraham when God promised that through him "all the families of the earth shall be blessed" (3:8; Gen. 12:3). That is, through Abraham the full contents of the gospel offer would be made possible for all families and nations of the earth.

The contents of this gospel offer as specified in this passage are the same basic elements of the "double cure" mentioned in several other places and discussed in some detail in connection with Acts 2:38. The first element is forgiveness or justification. Just as

Abraham was justified (counted righteous) by faith, God promised that He "would justify the Gentiles by faith" also (3:6,8).
The other element is the gift of the Holy Spirit, which was not
enjoyed by Abraham himself but was a major part of the blessing
that would come to others through him. This is seen in Galatians
3:2-5 and 4:6, and especially in 3:14, where "the blessing of
Abraham" is equated with "the promise of the Spirit."

These gospel gifts are described as "the blessing of Abraham"
(3:14), as "the promises . . . spoken to Abraham" (3:16), and
especially as "the inheritance" which Abraham was given the privilege of leaving to his offspring or heirs (3:18).

Now, the main question that arises at this point is this: *who* are
Abraham's *heirs*? Who will inherit these gospel blessings? To put
it another way, who is considered to be a *son* of Abraham?[2]
Sonship is the crucial idea. It is essential to have the status of a
son, since in the Old Testament economy ordinarily only sons
could inherit the family assets. As long as any sons were living,
women and slaves did not receive an inheritance. Only if there
were no sons could the daughters be heirs (Num. 27:1-11; 36:1-
12), and only if there were no natural heirs at all could slaves be
designated to inherit the property (Gen. 15:3). Thus to be an *heir*
of Abraham, one must be a *son* of Abraham. Until we are sons,
our status is no different from that of slaves (4:1-7): we have no
claim to the inheritance.[3]

At this stage in the argument Paul makes the very unexpected
point that Abraham has only one true son and heir, namely, Jesus
Christ (3:16). He notes that the promises were given to Abraham
and to his *seed*, singular. They are not given to many
*seeds*, plural, but just to the one seed or offspring,
which is Christ. Technically speaking He is the only
seed "to whom the promise had been made" (3:19).
Thus He is the only true son and heir of Abraham. The rest of us,
whether Jew or Gentile, slave or free, male or female, all seem to
be left out.

> Abraham has only one true son and heir, namely, Jesus Christ.

But here is where the gospel, the good news, gets even better.

Though Christ is the only true son and heir, *anyone* who is "in Christ Jesus" (3:14) or united with Christ is counted as a part of Christ Himself and therefore as a son and therefore as an heir! This is the main point of Galatians 3:26-29. Of course, Jesus is still the only natural son; the rest of us are sons by adoption (4:5).

Since being united with Christ is our only hope of receiving the gospel blessings, our main concern should thus be *how to become one mth Christ.* As we have already seen in our study of Romans 6:3-4, and as we shall see below, *baptism* marks our entry into this union.

## Clothed with Christ

Before we turn to the discussion of baptism itself, we must explore the meaning of the expression "clothed with Christ" as it appears in Galatians 3:27, "For all of you who were baptized into Christ have clothed yourselves with Christ." The imagery itself is quite vivid. Christ is compared with a garment that we put on and begin to wear at our baptism. But what does the image represent?

This same image or figure of speech is found in other places in Scripture besides here. Its meaning varies according to the context. Sometimes it seems to be equivalent to the second part of the double cure, to the "putting on" of a new nature through regeneration and a working out of that new nature in sanctification. We put off the old sinful self (Rom. 6:6) and put on a new holy one (Eph. 4:22-24). In a sense this "new self" is none other than Christ Himself, as Paul exhorts us to "put on the Lord Jesus Christ" (Rom. 13:14). "It is no longer I who live, but Christ lives in me," says Paul of himself (Gal. 2:20). The point is that we "put on Christ" when we are living in obedience to God's will by the power of Christ working in us and according to the example of His life.

Another possible meaning of "clothed with Christ" relates the image to the first part of the double cure, or justification. The key verse here is Isaiah 61:10, "I will rejoice greatly in the Lord, my

**99**

soul will exult in my God; for He has clothed me with garments of salvation, He has wrapped me with a robe of righteousness." In contrast to the "filthy garment" of our own futile "righteous deeds" (Isa. 64:6), God gives us the gift of His own righteousness to cover us like an all-encompassing robe. This is the "righteousness of God" which the New Testament makes central to the gospel (Rom. 1:16-17; 3:21; 10:3; 2 Cor. 5:21; Phil. 3:9). This "righteousness of God" is nothing less than the blood of Christ, by which He satisfied the righteous demands of God's law by paying the penalty for our sins. Thus to be "clothed with Christ" in this sense means to be covered by His blood as if it were a "robe of righteousness" covering all our sin.

Both of these aspects of salvation are included in the total Biblical concept of "putting on Christ" or being "clothed with Christ." It is doubtful, however, if either is specifically in view in Galatians 3:27. In view of the context it is most likely that the main point Paul wants to get across with this image is simply *union with Christ* in and of itself. When we are clothed with Christ, we are identified with Him; we are in Him; in a sense we are a very part of Him. What is true of Christ in a sense becomes true of us, too. The whole point of this is that because we are one with Christ, we share his sonship and heirship with regard to the blessing of Abraham. Indeed, this is the *only* way we can share in these things.

> When we are clothed with Christ, we are identified with Him.

The two following verses (3:28-29) confirm this understanding. Verse 28 says that all who are clothed with Christ are "one in [*en*] Christ Jesus." The word *in* is the Greek preposition *en*, which can also be translated "with" or "by." In my opinion it should be translated "with" in Galatians 3:28, so that it reads "you are all one *mth* Christ Jesus." This is the idea demanded by the context; the whole point is that we have been united with Christ, that we are one with Christ. Verse 29 affirms this union in still another way, by stating that "you *belong to* Christ." Then follows the conclusion to which all of this has been leading. *If* you belong to Christ (are clothed with Him, are one with Him), "then you are Abraham's offspring, heirs according to promise" (3:29). It does not matter if you are a Gentile, or a woman, or a slave — none of whom could inherit property according to Old Testament law. If you are in Christ and one with Him, you will be *treated* like a *son* and therefore will receive the inheritance anyway. This is summed up in 4:7, "Therefore you are no longer a slave, but a son; and if a son, then an heir through God."

## Faith, Baptism, and Sonship

Now we return to the question raised at the end of the section "Sons of God" above. According to this passage, *how* does anyone become clothed with Christ or united with Christ, and thus share in His sonship and inheritance? The two conditions specified here are *faith* and *baptism*.

The primary requirement for sharing in the Abrahamic inheritance is faith. This is one of the main themes of the book of Galatians. Apparently the churches of Galatia were under pressure from the group known as the Judaizers to include circumcision in the list of requirements for becoming a Christian. Since circumcision was the primary symbol of the whole Mosaic law, this was equivalent to requiring obedience to law as a condition for receiving saving grace — an impossible contradiction. Throughout this third

> The primary requirement for sharing in the Abrahamic inheritance is faith.

chapter especially, Paul stresses the contrast between the law-system of salvation, in which one is saved by his works, and the grace-system, in which one is saved by faith. "This is the only thing I want to find out from you," he says to the Galatian Christians: "Did you receive the Spirit by the works of the Law, or by hearing with faith?" (3:2; see 3:5). The inheritance is not received by legal conditions (and thus by works), but by faith in God's gracious promises (3:14,18,22).

This is the background for the crucial statement in Galatians 3:26, "For you are all sons of God through faith in Christ Jesus." Here "sons of God" is no different from "sons of Abraham"

(3:7); the inheritance is through Abraham but is ultimately from God. The important point is sonship itself, since only sons can be heirs. How do we become sons? Through *faith* in Christ Jesus.

This is highly appropriate, since Abraham's own acceptance with God was through faith. "Even so Abraham believed God, and it was reckoned to him as righteousness" (3:6; see Gen. 15:6). That is, through his faith he was *justified*. As "Abraham the believer" (3:9) he is a model for anyone who wants to be adopted into his family. Only when we imitate his faith can we be his sons: "Therefore, be sure that it is those who are of faith that are sons of Abraham" (3:7). Only when we imitate his faith can we be his heirs: "So then those who are of faith are blessed with Abraham, the believer" (3:9). Like Abraham, we too are "justified by faith" (3:24).

It is not just a question of what is *appropiate*, however, as if inclusion in Abraham's family were merely an apt or suitable reward for someone who imitates his faith. We cannot forget Paul's point that only *one* "seed" or son is a rightful heir to the Abrahamic promises (3:16), and that son is Christ. A faith like Abraham's does not in and of itself bestow upon us the status of sonship, *but it does bring us into union with Christ*, and *this* is what includes us in Abraham's family. "If you *belong to Christ*, then you are Abraham's offspring, heirs according to promise" (3:29). We must not forget the Christological focus of our faith nor the Christological basis of the inheritance itself.

Verse 26 is very clear that faith is necessary for the status of sonship: we are "sons of God *through faith*." But verse 27 is just as clear that *baptism* is the action that unites us with Christ, thus making our sonship possible: "for all of you who were baptized into Christ have clothed yourselves with Christ." The expression *baptized into Christ* is the same as that in Romans 6:3. We saw in that discussion how the idea of "into Christ," with the Greek preposition *eis*, refers to the event of entering into union with Christ. According to both Romans 6:3 and Galatians 3:27, the action that brings this about is baptism: we are *baptized* into Christ.

Galatians makes this connection between baptism and union with Christ even more emphatic when it says that baptism into Christ is equivalent to clothing yourselves with Christ. The concepts are almost equated. If you have done one, says Paul, then you have done the other. If you have been baptized into Christ, then you have clothed yourselves with Christ. They are practically the same thing.

The concepts are *almost* equated, but not quite. More precisely, they are brought into such a close cause-and-effect relationship that we cannot separate them. Being clothed with Christ is the necessary result or effect of being baptized into Christ. This is the point of the sequence of the ideas in the verse.

The sequence of the concepts is worth noting for another reason. We may remember that the common Protestant understanding of baptism is that it is an act that *follows* the reception of salvation in order to symbolize the fact that one has *already* become one with Christ. But if this were true, the order of Galatians 3:27 would have to be just the opposite: "all of you who were clothed with Christ were then baptized into Christ." But this is not what it says, because this is not the way it happens. It is the other way around, as the verse indicates.

How can we be sure this verse is speaking of *water* baptism, though? Could it be referring to Holy Spirit baptism, and not to water baptism at all? As we saw in the last chapter, this kind of distinction is not Biblically valid; there is only "one baptism" (Eph. 4:5). When the Galatians who originally received Paul's letter read this statement about their own baptism, only one event would have entered their minds: their immersion in water for the forgiveness of sins and the gift of the Holy Spirit.

Verse 26 speaks of *becoming sons* through faith; verse 27 speaks of *being united with Christ* through baptism. How are these concepts related? Are they the same thing, or is there just a logical (if not chronological) sequence in view? The answer is that they are not the same, but again are so closely related as cause and effect that they cannot be separated. That is, the sonship in verse 26 is the effect of the union with Christ in verse 27. Verse 26 affirms that we *are* sons of God through faith, and verse 27 explains *how* this came about. The key is the word *for* (Greek, *gar*) at the beginning of verse 27, which has the force of *because*. We are sons of God through faith, *because* we have been baptized into Christ. Union with Christ is the cause or prerequisite of sonship.

> Since union with Christ is entered into at baptism, then baptism also is a prerequisite of sonship.

And since union with Christ is entered into at baptism, then baptism also is a prerequisite of sonship.

There is a further significance of this for baptism: that which happens in baptism is the prerequisite of that which is said to happen through faith. We are sons of God through faith, but this sonship is not acquired *as soon as* we have faith. Rather, it is acquired when this faith leads us into the baptism which unites us with Christ. This should serve as a caution against the common error of equating the Biblical expression "through faith" with the quite different concept "as soon as we have faith." As an analogy, having ten dollars may be a necessary prerequisite for getting into the ball park and seeing the ball game, but this does not mean that one will see the ball game as soon as he has the ten dollars. He still has to go to the place where the ball game is being played. Likewise, having faith is a necessary prerequisite for sonship and thus heirship, but we still have to go to the place where this sonship is bestowed, which is baptism.

This does not detract at all from the significance of faith, but rather simply shows the strong bond and affinity between faith and baptism, a fact that was pointed out in our discussion of Mark 16:16.

This affinity between faith and baptism is underscored all the more by the fact that such a strong statement affirming the saving significance of baptism appears in a context where a law-system (salvation by works) is contrasted with the grace-system (salvation by faith in God's promises). In the book of Galatians as a whole and in chapter 3 especially, Paul is attacking the idea that a sinner can be saved by works of law — especially the Law of Moses, and especially the work of circumcision.[4] But in this very context where salvation by works is condemned, salvation (specifically union with Christ) by baptism is affirmed. This shows that baptism is not to be considered as a work, viz., as an act of obedience done simply because God as Lawgiver has commanded it. It is instead a vital part of the grace-system itself. That is, baptism is itself a work of divine grace in which the human side has the character of faith rather than works.

A final point concerning baptism is the relationship between it and circumcision. Baptism is commonly regarded as the New Testament successor to Old Testament circumcision; it is seen as having the same basic relation to the New Covenant as circumcision had to the Old Covenant. A moment's reflection, however, on the way circumcision is treated here in Galatians as opposed to the way baptism is regarded, should dispel the notion that they are in any way equivalent. Circumcision is rejected not because it has been replaced by baptism[5] but because *no* mere work of human obedience can be a prerequisite for receiving grace. Circumcision is such a work and thus is excluded from the conditions for receiving grace, and is excluded in the harshest of terms. Baptism, on the other hand, is linked with faith and is spoken of quite naturally as that which brings us into saving union with Christ and thus into sonship and heirship themselves. A contrast more pronounced than this would be difficult to imagine; the discontinuity between circumcision and baptism is thus quite complete.[6]

# Summary

In this consideration of Galatians 3:26-27 we have discussed first of all the general context, which is dealing with the question of who may inherit the blessing of Abraham. Who are Abraham's sons and heirs? Actually there is only one true son, Jesus Christ. But the good news is that anyone who is *in Christ* is also counted as a son and thus as an heir of the gospel promises.

We have also discussed the meaning of the term "clothed with Christ." In some contexts it refers to imitating Christ in holy living, namely, sanctification. Another understanding is that it refers to our being covered with the blood of Christ as with a "robe of righteousness," or justification. In Galatians 3:27, however, it seems to have the more general significance of union with Christ as such. To be clothed with Christ means to be one with Him and thus to be treated as He is treated, namely, as a son and heir.

Finally we have discussed how faith and baptism are related to sonship. They are specified here as the two basic conditions for becoming one with Christ and thus sons and heirs with Him.

> Baptism is thus embraced together with faith in the grace-system.

Baptism itself is the specific point where we become one with Christ or clothed with Him. Union with Christ logically follows baptism as its precondition — not vice versa, as many think. Likewise, becoming sons of God through faith (3:26) logically follows becoming one with Christ in baptism (3:27). That which happens *through faith* does not happen *until baptism*. Baptism is thus embraced together with faith in the grace-system, and is not a work of law like circumcision. The contrasting ways in which baptism and circumcision are treated in Galatians show that baptism cannot be the New Testament equivalent of circumcision.

## NOTES

1. In this chapter, the numerous Scripture references where the book of the Bible is not named are from Galatians 3 and 4.

2. In this context there seems to be no difference between a "son of Abraham" (3:7) and a "son of God" (3:26).

3. This is the sole idea that underlies the three contrasts in the much-vexed passage, Galatians 3:28. According to Jewish law, only *free Jewish males* could inherit property. Greeks or Gentiles could not be heirs, nor could slaves or females (in most circumstances). The only thing at stake here is who can inherit the blessing of Abraham.

4. On the contrast between law and grace (and thus works and faith) in Galatians, see 2:16,21; 3:2,5; 5:4. On the futility of seeking salvation by lawkeeping, see 3:10-13; 4:21ff. On the condemnation of circumcision as a requirement for salvation, see 2:2-5; 5:2-3,11; 6:12-15.

5. If circumcision *had* been replaced by baptism, this would have been the logical context to make that point clear. It would have been the strongest argument against
   the Judaizers, those who wanted to make circumcision a part of the gospel. But
   there is total silence in Galatians about such a connection. There *is* no such
   connection.

6. The relation between baptism and circumcision will be discussed further in connection with Colossians 2:12. See below.

# ⧼ **10** ⧽
# EPHESIANS 5:25-27

nother reference to baptism in Paul's epistles is Ephesians 5:26, where he refers to "the washing of water with the word." This is in the middle of a longer statement about the relationship between Christ and His church. The full statement (5:25-27) is as follows:

> Husbands, love your wives, just as Christ also loved the church and gave Himself up for her; that He might sanctify her, having cleansed her by the washing of water with the word, that He might present to Himself the church in all her glory, having no spot or wrinkle or any such thing; but that she should be holy and blameless.

This passage is basically talking about what Christ has done to rid His church of sin, and it shows that baptism has a central part to play in this process.

## A Sanctified Church

The end result of Christ's work is that He might have for Himself a sanctified church. This point is made in the midst of a discussion of the ideal relationship between husbands and wives. The main exhortation for the wife is that she should be subject to the headship of the husband (5:22-24). From the standpoint of the husband, the most important thing he can do is to love his wife (5:25,28-29).

> The end result of Christ's work is that He might have for Himself a sanctified church.

The model for both husband and wife is the relationship between Christ and His church, both His headship over it and His

**109**

love for it. The latter is our main concern here. Husbands should love their wives just as Christ loved the church. Just how much did He love her? He loved her so much that He made the greatest possible sacrifice that love can make (John 15:13): He "gave Himself up for her" (5:25). This is a reference to the saving death of Christ, in which He took our place and suffered the wrath of God which we deserve. It refers to the cross upon which Christ in love gave Himself up as an atoning sacrifice, taking our sin and its penalty upon Himself.

What was Christ's purpose for "giving Himself up" in this way? The answer is stated in two ways. First, He gave Himself for the church "that He might sanctify her" (5:26). Second, He gave Himself "that He might present to Himself the church in all her glory, having no spot or wrinkle or any such thing; but that she should be holy and blameless" (5:27). It may be that these are just two ways of saying the same thing, with the second statement being an elaboration of the first. Or it may be that the first of these purposes, "that He might sanctify her," refers to the sanctifying *action* of Christ as such, while the second refers to the *result* of that action, which is the *state* of sanctification. The former would be the cause, and the latter the effect. Christ gave Himself up that He might sanctify the church, with the goal in mind of her complete purity and holiness as His bride and wife. Verse 27 alludes to the visual picture of "a bride adorned for her husband" (Rev. 21:2) in a wedding dress so glorious and perfect that it has " no spot or wrinkle." This visual picture is an analogy or a figure of Christ's goal for His church, that she might stand before Him in perfect *moral* purity, "holy and blameless." In other words, He desires a *sanctified* church.

Exactly what is sanctification? The Biblical verbs for this concept basically mean "to cut, to separate, to set apart." The word *holy* and related terms are synonyms for *sanctified* and other such terms. The following are equivalent translations: verbs, "to sanctify" and "to make holy"; nouns, "holiness" and "sanctification";

more nouns, "holy one," "sanctified one," and "saint"; and adjectives, "holy" and "sanctified."

The fundamental pattern for speaking of human holiness or sanctification is the holiness of God, who is holy in two distinct ways. First, God is holy in the sense that He is separate or distinct from His creation; He is a different kind of being, an uncreated and infinite being. As Creator, He is set apart from His creation; He transcends it. We call this His *ontological* holiness. Second, God is holy in the sense that He is separate from all sin. He has not sinned and cannot sin; He is totally opposed to all sin in every way. He exists eternally and unchangeably in complete moral purity. We call this His *moral* holiness.

In reference to human beings the terms *holiness* and *sanctification* are used to describe an aspect of our salvation. They refer to the second part of the "double cure," our deliverance from the presence and power of sin in our lives. As applied to our salvation this concept seems to have two distinct senses, corresponding to the two aspects of divine holiness.

First, the Christian is holy (has been sanctified) in the sense that he has been *set apart* from the world as it now exists, namely, "this present evil age" (Gal. 1:4) that has been corrupted by sin and stands under God's curse. We no longer belong to that old creation, but have been made a part of the new creation (2 Cor. 5:17). We are physically *in* this world, but are not *of* this world (John 17:11-16). "For He delivered us from the domain of darkness, and transferred us to the kingdom of His beloved Son" (Col. 1:13). This is called *initial* sanctification because it occurs at the very beginning of our Christian life as a single, completed act. This is that to which the aorist verb in 1 Corinthians 6:11 refers, "you were sanctified" as a past completed act.

The act of sanctification in Ephesians 5:26 must include at least this initial sanctification.[1] It is an act of Jesus Christ — "that *He* might sanctify her." It is a direct purpose and result of His atoning death; He gave Himself up *in order that* He might sanctify the church. As Hebrews 10:10 says, "We have been sanctified

**111**

through the offering of the body of Jesus Christ once for all." Hebrews 13:12 reaffirms this point, saying that Jesus suffered on the cross "that He might sanctify the people through His own blood" (see Heb. 10:29). Because we have been "baptized into His death" (Rom. 6:3), His atoning blood covers the church and sets it apart from the world. Those to whom the blood of Christ has been applied are by that very fact given a unique status as "a holy nation, a people for God's own possession" (1 Pet. 2:9). They are already "saints" (sanctified ones), not because they are perfect but because they are forgiven by His blood.

The second sense in which a Christian is sanctified (holy) is that he is set apart from sin itself. The desire to sin is removed from the heart; sinful habits are overcome; sinful thoughts and deeds are excluded from daily life. Unlike initial sanctifica-

> The desire to sin is removed from the heart; sinful habits are overcome; sinful thoughts and deeds are excluded from daily life.

tion, this does not happen all at once but is a continuing process over the course of the Christian life. Thus it is called *progressive* sanctification. It means becoming more and more like God in His own moral holiness: "Like the Holy One who called you, be holy yourselves also in all your behavior; because it is written, 'You shall be holy, for I am holy'" (1 Pet. 1:15-16).

This aspect of our sanctification is also made possible by the death of Christ. As we saw in our discussion of Romans 6:3-4, Christ died to destroy the power of sin and do away with it forever. When we are baptized into His death, we too experience a death to sin, which along with our union with Christ in His resurrection implants within us the very possibility of defeating sin in our own lives. Also, once He had completed His work of death and resurrection, Jesus earned the right to send forth the promised Holy Spirit (Acts 2:33), whose continuing presence in our lives provides the ongoing power for overcoming sin. This is "the sanctifying work of the Spirit" (1 Pet. 1:2).

Since both aspects of sanctification are thus based upon the death of Christ, it is likely that Ephesians 5:26 includes both as the purpose for which Christ "gave Himself up." Obviously the end result described in verse 27 is the ultimate goal of progressive sanctification. Some take this verse as a reference to our being *justified* by Christ's blood, namely, our being clothed with the "robe of righteousness," as discussed in relation to Galatians 3:27. It is true that this is the *only* way we can be " holy and blameless" before Him until the process of sanctification is complete. But though this is sufficient for our salvation, Christ is not satisfied with this alone, and neither should we be. He wants us to be *actually* holy and blameless before Him, completely separate from sin in every respect. Though this will probably not come to pass until after our death and resurrection[2] and only then by a special gift of God, there *will* come a time when we are completely freed from sin and are fully sanctified. When the church as bride finally is presented to Christ at the marriage supper in heaven, it will be "given to her to clothe herself in fine linen, bright and clean; for the fine linen is the righteous acts of the saints" (Rev. 19:8).

Surely, if it is Christ's desire as a loving Bridegroom to want His bride to be as holy and pure as possible, then this should be our deepest desire, too. If we truly love the Bridegroom, we should be doing everything we can even now to rid ourselves of every "spot or wrinkle." If He has given His own life to bring it about, how can we give less than our best effort?

## A Cleansed Church

Thus far we have concentrated on the idea of sanctification and have ignored the reference in Ephesians 5:26 to Christ's *cleansing* of the church. Christ gave Himself up for the church, says Paul, "that He might sanctify her, *having cleansed her.*" What does this mean, and how is it related to sanctification?

The Greek word translated "cleansed" means "to cleanse from dirt or any impurity, to purify." It and other words in the same family can refer to cleansing from physical dirt (Matt. 23:25-26), from ritual uncleanness (Luke 2:22), and from disease (Mark

**113**

1:40-42). But these words can and often do refer to *spiritual* cleansing. Sometimes the reference is to sanctification, the cleansing from actual sin described in the previous section. This is true of the many passages about the "pure in heart," e.g., Matthew 5:8; 1 Timothy 1:5. See also 2 Corinthians 7:1, "Let us cleanse ourselves from all defilement of flesh and spirit, perfecting holiness in the fear of God." Some argue that this is its meaning here in Ephesians 5:26, and that it is synonymous with sanctification.

But sometimes when this word group refers to spiritual cleansing, it means *justification,* or cleansing from the *guilt* of sin. This seems to be true especially of references to cleansing with blood, where the Old Testament background of using the blood of sacrificed animals in ritual cleansing ceremonies was symbolic of forgiveness.[3] The two are tied together in Hebrews 9:22, which says that according to the Law "all things are cleansed with blood, and without shedding of blood there is no *forgiveness*" (see Heb. 1:3). In my opinion this is what it means in Ephesians 5:26. It is not the same as sanctification, but is the necessary precondition of it. Because Christ has already forgiven His church, viz., cleansed her from her guilt. He can now sanctify her. A cleansed church is thus free to be a sanctified church.[4]

> A cleansed church is free to be a sanctified church.

The most important part of this passage from the standpoint of our present study is what Paul says about the *means* of the church's cleansing. In other texts various elements are named as indispensable for this cleansing. These include faith (Acts 15:9), the word *(logos,* John 15:3), and the blood of Christ (1 John 1:7). Without a doubt the last of these, the blood of Christ, is the one thing that provides the inherent power for our cleansing, the one thing that is applied directly to our souls for the washing away of sin. But this fact makes neither faith nor the word superfluous; they each have a necessary part to play in the actual applying of the cleansing blood (see Rom. 10:13-17). But what about Ephesians 5:26? It says that the church is cleansed "by the washing of water with the word." Whatever this "washing of water" is, it too plays a necessary part in the application of Christ's cleansing blood to the guilty soul.

What is the "washing of water"? There can be little question that it refers to baptism. The Greek word for "washing" is *loutron*, which can mean "washing" or "bath." It is used for baptism in Titus 3:5. It is a noun form of the verb *louo*, which also is used in other places for baptism.[5] The idea that it is used here figuratively for some purely spiritual bath is precluded by the reference to water; it is the "washing *of water.*" The only "washing of water" in Christian experience is baptism. It is noteworthy that definite articles are used with both "washing" and "water," namely, "by *the* washing of *the* water," the specific water of baptism. The fact that it is a "washing of water *with the word*" also points to baptism, since "the word" is a prominent aspect of baptism. Indeed, the only place where water and word are combined in our Christian faith is in baptism.

The Greek term for "word" is *rema* (pronounced RAY-ma), which means specifically the *spoken* word. This could refer to the confession of Christ which is usually connected with baptism (see Rom. 10:9-10), or the "calling on His name" discussed in the study of Acts 22:16. More likely it refers to the word spoken by God rather than men, specifically the Great Commission (Matt. 28:19) or the word of promise as stated in passages such as Mark 16:16 (see the earlier studies of these texts).

## Baptism and the Church

Just how important is baptism? This passage shows that it is part of the very foundation of the church's experience of salvation. Verse 26 presents this sequence of dependence: the church's *sanctification* rests upon its *cleansing* (or justification), which in turn rests upon *baptism.* The cleansing and the sanctification are the very essence of salvation, and they begin in baptism.

> The cleansing and the sanctification are the very essence of salvation, and they begin in baptism.

Is such a strong connection between baptism and the church's salvation warranted by this passage? It is if we remain true to the language itself. The view is commonly voiced that baptism only demonstrates or illustrates or visually represents the spiritual cleansing attributed to baptism, but there is nothing in the text itself that suggests such a mere figurative connection. In the text the Greek word for "washing" is in the dative case and modifies "cleansing." In such an expression the dative case has the meaning of what is called the "dative of means." That is, it indicates the *means* by which the described action takes place. To be very precise, the text says that the church is cleansed *by means of baptism* as connected with the word. Anyone who does not like this way of speaking should complain to the Apostle Paul and to the Holy Spirit who inspired him.

Someone will surely ask, if we are cleansed by baptism, what is the need for the blood of Christ? Does baptism somehow take the place of Christ's blood? May it never be! As stated in the previous section, the only thing that can literally and directly cleanse the sinner's heart is the blood of Jesus Christ. The water of baptism in no way touches the soul or washes the soul; let no one accuse us of affirming such a metaphysical impossibility. Nevertheless we must do justice to what Paul says here in Ephesians 5:26, that we are cleansed by baptism. What this must mean is that God has so united the divine act of cleansing the soul through Christ's blood with the "washing of water" (baptism) that the latter itself is spoken of *as if it were* the actual means. At the very least we must say this, that baptism is the means of spiritual cleansing in the sense that it is *the divinely appointed time* during which the cleansing takes place. This union of blood and water as simultaneous inner and outer cleansings is affirmed in Hebrews 10:22, which says that we have had "our hearts sprinkled clean from an evil conscience and our bodies washed with pure water" (the conscience is cleansed by the blood of Christ — Hebrews 9:14).

What unites the blood of Christ and the water of baptism into a single event of such grace and power? No less than the *word of*

**116**

*God*. The washing of water by which we are cleansed is not just *any* water, but the water of baptism, which is given its efficacy only by the precious word of God, the spoken word of God's promises which all ultimately rest upon the shed blood of Christ. Why should baptism have such power? In itself it does not; the power comes only through God's appointment. He has so declared it, and His word is enough! In our baptism our faith penetrates behind and beyond the water in order to lay hold of the cleansing blood of Christ. But what carries it beyond the water? The word of promise! Of all the tangible elements of baptism, this is the only one that has any inherent power; this is what faith wraps itself around in baptism in order to grasp the blood itself. In the washing of water we find the word of promise, and in the word of promise we find the blood of Christ. What God has joined together, let no man put asunder.[6]

It should be noted that all the saving actions in this passage are the actions of Christ and not of any human agent. Christ loved the church; Christ gave Himself for the church; Christ sanctified the church; Christ cleansed the church; Christ presents the church to Himself in glorious holiness. Whatever saving activity happens in baptism is not the work of the baptizer or the one baptized, but the work of Christ Himself. Like a loving husband He does whatever is necessary to make His bride the church whole and pure. If He deems it appropriate to do part of this work in the act of baptism, that is His prerogative as Head of the church and as the Lord of salvation itself. As His submissive bride our only proper choice is to yield to His headship and allow Him to work His works of salvation according to *His* will.

> All the saving actions in this passage are the actions of Christ and not of any human agent.

We cannot forget that what Christ has done for us in baptism required His previous sacrifice on the cross. He first gave Himself up for the church (5:25) to make it possible to sanctify and cleanse her by the washing of water (5:26). In view of this we must constantly ask ourselves, what are *we* willing to do now to cleanse ourselves of daily sin?

**117**

# Summary

In this study of Ephesians 5:25-27 we have seen first of all how Christ has *sanctified* and is sanctifying His church. This includes *initial* sanctification, in which sinners are called out from the world and are set apart into a new creation at conversion. It also includes *progressive* sanctification, in which Christians continue to eradicate sin from their lives and become more and more holy. Christ's goal for such sanctification is that He might have a pure and holy bride.

We have also seen how this sanctification presupposes that Christ has *cleansed* the church. Though some equate this with sanctification itself, it more likely refers to how Christ has justified or forgiven us through His blood. Though His blood is the true and literal means of this cleansing, verse 26 says we are cleansed *by the washing of water,* which is baptism. Connected with this washing is the spoken word of God, His word of promise.

Finally we have seen in some detail how this passage connects baptism very closely with our salvation in a foundational way. Our sanctification rests on our cleansing, and this cleansing rests upon the washing of water, viz., baptism. Though only the blood of Christ truly cleanses the soul, it has been so united with baptism by the word of God that the baptism itself can be spoken of as if it were the means of cleansing. It is so in the sense that it is the divinely-appointed *time* when the sinner is cleansed by the blood.

## NOTES

1. The verb in Ephesians 5:26, "that He might sanctify her," is aorist, leading some to believe that this refers *only* to initial sanctification. The manner of speaking in this verse does not require this limitation, however.

2. Church groups in the Wesleyan tradition usually embrace the doctrine that complete sanctification is possible and should be sought even in this life.

3. See the discussion of Old Testament washing ceremonies in the discussion of Acts 2:38 above.

4. The fact that "cleansed" is an aorist participle modifying "sanctify" may have some bearing on this point. Usually a *present* participle is used for action that occurs

at the same time as that of the main verb, while an *aorist* participle stands for action that occurs *before* that of the main verb. If this rule applies here, and I think it does, then the cleansing takes place before the sanctifying and is a separate act. The priority may be more logical than chronological, however, with no real time separating the two acts. (Some argue that an aorist participle does not *have* to refer to action preceding that of the main verb but may describe action simultaneous to that of the main verb.)

5. See the discussion of "wash away your sins" in the study of Acts 22:16 above. See the full article by Oepke on *louo,* cited above in Chapter 7, footnote 3. With the exception of a few clearly secular uses, says Oepke, "all others are related to freeing from sin, and esp. to baptism" (p. 302). This includes Eph. 5:26.

6. Oepke (in the work just cited in the previous footnote) says this: "The cleansing takes place through the specified bath (double art.) by means of the word. The word is that spoken at baptism. This word brings the preceding word of proclamation to its goal. It is neither to be perverted into magic nor dissolved into mere symbolism. It goes back to God and Christ, and thence derives its efficacy" (304).

# ≈11≈
# COLOSSIANS 2:11-13

n my opinion a good case can be made that Colossians 2:11-13 is the most important New Testament passage concerning baptism. It reads thus:

> And in Him you were also circumcised with a circumcision made without hands, in the removal of the body of the flesh by the circumcision of Christ; having been buried with Him in baptism, in which you were also raised up with Him through faith in the working of God, who raised Him from the dead. And when you were dead in your transgressions and the uncircumcision of your flesh. He made you alive together with Him, having forgiven us all our transgressions.

One reason this passage is so important is because it most explicitly identifies baptism as the specific time when a sinner is buried with Christ and raised up with Him. Another is because it most explicitly spells out the distinctive roles of faith and baptism in the reception of salvation. Also, it clearly indicates that insofar as baptism is a work, it is a work of God. Also, it gives us the only New Testament teaching on how to relate baptism and circumcision. Finally, it supplements and completes the teaching on salvation found in its parallel passage, Ephesians 2:1-10.[1] These points will now be discussed in more detail.

## Buried in Baptism

In many ways the content of this passage echoes that of Romans 6:3-6. The most explicit parallel is the concept of being buried with Christ in baptism. Romans 6:4 says that "we have been buried with Him through baptism into death"; Colossians 2:12 also speaks of our "having been buried with Him in baptism." The wording is identical except that Romans uses the preposition *through (dia)* while Colossians uses *in (en)*. Other parallels are quite evident though not as explicit.

Thus Colossians, like Romans, affirms that baptism is a burial *with Christ*. Because of the similarity with Romans we can readily infer that this means baptism is a burial with Christ *into His death*. What is the significance of this? What is the result of it? We might conclude that it results in forgiveness of sins, since burial into Christ's death would bring us into saving contact with the justifying blood of Jesus. Verse 13 specifically relates forgiveness to this event when it refers to God's "having forgiven us all our transgressions." This understanding of baptism as the time of forgiveness certainly agrees with passages such as Acts 2:38 and Acts 22:16.

But, as is the case with Romans, the primary emphasis here seems to be on regeneration or the new birth rather than forgiveness as such. Here again the idea of a burial implies an accompanying death, namely, our own death to sin which precedes our resurrection to newness of life. This death *to* sin is not the same as being dead *in* sins, a concept mentioned in verse 13 and discussed in the section "Raised Up in Baptism" below. Rather, what Romans 6 calls death *to* sin (6:11) is described in the Colossians passage under the figure of circumcision (2:11).

Verse 11 says we have been circumcised in a non-physical sense ("without hands"), that is, we have experienced a *spiritual* circumcision. This is called a "removal of the body of the flesh." This is similar to physical circumcision, which is the removal of a piece of the physical body. But in spiritual circumcision "the body of the flesh" refers to our old way of life or our old sinful nature, not the physical body as such or any part of it. In baptism this old sinful aspect of our being is circumcised away; it dies and is disposed of.

> In baptism this old sinful aspect of our being is circumcised away; it dies and is disposed of.

Herein lies the identification with Romans 6, where dying with Christ to sin means "that our old self was crucified with Him, that

**122**

our body of sin might be done away with" (6:6). The "old self" (literally, "old man") and the "body of sin" in Romans are the same as "the body of the flesh" in Colossians. In baptism, by the power of the death of Christ with which we are thus united, this old self is put to death and put off (removed) in a spiritual act analogous to physical circumcision, then left buried in the waters of baptism. (See also Colossians 2:13, which refers to the sinner's condition as a state of "the uncircumcision of your flesh."[2])

When Colossians 2:12 says this takes place "in baptism," it is affirming what the whole New Testament assumes and teaches, namely, that baptism is an act of salvation. It does not say this happens "before baptism" or "after baptism," but specifically and clearly *in baptism*. This shows that we must at least say that baptism is the time or occasion during which God bestows salvation upon the sinner. The fact that "having been buried" is an aorist participle shows that this act (of baptism) *precedes* or is at least simultaneous with the act of spiritual circumcision in verse 11.

Though baptism is thus accorded a very high place in the plan of salvation, we must emphasize that it does not take the place of Christ and His saving blood. Indeed the focus of this passage, like all other Biblical teaching about baptism, is upon Jesus Christ. Baptism brings about this spiritual circumcision only because in it we are buried *with Christ*. It is still His power, the power of His death, that accomplishes this saving deed. Indeed, verse 11 calls it "the circumcision of Christ." This means it is a circumcision accomplished *by* Christ and His divine power, not a circumcision accomplished *upon* Christ, as some want to interpret it. More importantly, it is something *He* does to us and for us, not something we do for ourselves.

We may briefly note here, as with Romans 6, that the description of the action of baptism as a *burial* simply reinforces the fact that baptism is immersion. Though it is proper to emphasize this from Colossians 2:12, however, we must remember that this is not the main point of referring to baptism as a burial. The main point is that baptism is a *spiritual* burial into union with Christ,

**123**

by virtue of which our "old self" is given a deathblow and is left behind as in a grave when we are raised up with Christ into new life. The same applies to baptism as a spiritual resurrection. We must not be so eager to prove immersion from this text that we overlook this deeper level of divine activity which is taking place within our souls even as our bodies are being immersed into the water and raised up therefrom.

## Raised Up in Baptism

This reference to baptism as a spiritual resurrection leads to our next point, namely, that Colossians 2:12 affirms that baptism is the time during which we are "raised up with Him." This too echoes Romans 6, where union with Christ includes participating in the power of His resurrection. See also Ephesians 2:5-6 and Colossians 3:1, which have the same language. In keeping with the meaning of Romans 6, this means that a new being, a new creation arose from the water-grave of baptism, to take the place of the old self that died in baptism. Thus baptism is both a death and a resurrection.

Here in Colossians, however, "raised up in baptism" has a connotation that is not explicit in Romans 6. There is another sense in which baptism is a resurrection from the dead, because there is another sense in which we have experienced death itself. That is, there is another kind of death from which we are raised in baptism. These two kinds of death must be clearly distinguished.

The first kind of death is the one discussed in the section above, namely, death *to* sin. From this perspective the old sinful self is alive and well and in control until baptism, in which it is put to death (or circumcised away) and buried, and from which a new self is raised up to take its place. The other kind of death is death *in* sin. From this perspective the sinner is already dead; he has existed in a state of spiritual death from the moment he became a sinner. This is that to which Colossians 2:13 refers when it says "you were dead in your transgressions." As Ephesians 2:1 says, "You were dead in your trespasses and sins" (see 2:5).

**124**

To be dead in sin is not just being under the *penalty* of death, but rather being in an actual *state* or condition of death. The soul itself is dead and infested with spiritual decay in the form of evil thoughts, lust, jealousy, covetousness, hatred, and other sin. The sinner's will is too weak to overcome the power of sin and temptation on its own. His heart is hardened against God and blinded to His truth. He is caught in the "helpless weakness of sin" that makes him powerless to please God (Rom. 8:7-8).[3] This is the sense in which a person is already dead when he enters the waters of baptism.

> The sinner's will is too weak to overcome the power of sin and temptation on its own.

As part of the gospel offer, God promises to raise the sinner from this state of spiritual death. (This is the second half of the "double cure" again.) He promises to do this in Christian baptism, specifically through the gift of the Holy Spirit, whose special work is to "give life" (see John 6:63; 2 Cor. 3:6). This aspect of salvation is the same as the new birth or regeneration, but in this context it is described in the most forceful of terms, *resurrection from the dead*. Two different words are used in order to reinforce the dramatic nature of this act: you were "*raised up with him*" (Col. 2:12), and "He *made you alive* together with Him" (Col. 2:13). The parallel passage in Ephesians 2:5-6 says the same thing: "Even when we were dead in our transgressions," God "made us alive together with Christ . . . and raised us up with Him." Truly our Redeemer is a God "who gives life to the dead" (Rom. 4:17).

As Christians we need to realize that we once were dead in sin but have experienced a literal, though spiritual, resurrection from the dead. God can say of us as of the prodigal son, "This son of mine was dead, and has come to life again" (Luke 15:24). We have "passed out of death into life" (John 5:24). How can we doubt that this is the most significant thing that has *ever* happened to us? And when does Paul say it took place? *In baptism!* "Having been buried with Him in baptism, *in which* you were also raised up with Him" (Col. 2:12). The expression "in which" (Greek, *en ho*) follows in the text immediately after "in baptism" *(en to baptismati)*, and as a relative pronoun of the same gender must refer back to baptism.[4]

Thus again we see that Colossians 2:12 is probably the clearest and most specific New Testament testimony to the fact that the application of Christ's saving work to the sinner takes place *in baptism*. We are "raised up with Him" *in baptism*. Baptism is the time and place when the saving benefits of Christ's own death, burial, and resurrection are applied to us.

> The application of Christ's saving work to the sinner takes place in baptism.

## Faith in the Working of God

Another very important point in Colossians 2:12 is the relation between baptism and faith in God's plan of salvation. We are buried and raised up with Christ *in baptism* as the time and place, but *through faith* as the means. The role of faith is not negated by the designation of baptism as the time of salvation, nor is there any conflict between the two. Rather, they complement one another perfectly. (See the discussion of this point in the chapters on Mark 16:16 and Galatians 3:26-27 above.)

When Paul says we are buried and raised with Him *through faith*, this shows that going through the motions of baptism is not a true baptism *unless* the one being baptized has faith in his heart. There is no magical power in the water or in the act itself. Baptism without faith is a futile dipping in water. No burial into Christ accompanies the burial into the water; no resurrection with Christ accompanies the lifting out of the water. Without faith the person's spiritual state after baptism is no different from what it was before.

This has two important implications. First, the New Testament doctrine of baptism as explained here should not be confused with "baptismal regeneration" in the classical sense of that term. Strictly speaking the idea of baptismal regeneration as taught by some church groups (especially traditional Roman Catholicism and Anglicanism) means that the proper application of baptism automatically produces regeneration even in the absence of faith on the part of the recipient.[5] This would be especially true in the case of infant baptism as taught by these groups. But such "baptismal regeneration" is *not* the same as the Biblical teaching that regeneration occurs *during* baptism *but only when faith is also present.* It is very misleading and prejudicial to label the latter as "baptismal regeneration," especially when this term has so many negative connotations in most of Protestantism today.

The second implication of the way faith and baptism are related in Colossians 2:12 is that infant baptism is ruled out as true baptism. This is so for other reasons as well, but here it is made clear that only those sinners who are able to exercise true faith in Christ are proper subjects for baptism. Since infants cannot believe, it is futile to try to baptize them.[6]

Colossians 2:12 not only teaches the necessity of faith for a valid baptism but also describes what the specific object of this faith must be. It must be a "faith in the working of God, who raised Him from the dead." The Greek word for "working" is *energeia,* which means not just latent power but actual activity or active working. We must have faith in the "working of God," namely, in the reality of the deeds or works which God has done and promises to do for our redemption.

This means first of all that we must believe in what God has already done for us through Jesus Christ in His death and resurrection. We must believe that the cross was a mighty working of God in which He was taking away the sin of the world through the substitutionary death of His Son. We must also believe that God raised Jesus from the dead to defeat His enemies and to secure eternal life for us. This latter working is specifically mentioned in Colossians 2:12. We must believe in the working of God, *who raised Him (Jesus) from the dead.* (See Rom. 10:9.)

"Faith in the working of God" also means that in baptism we must believe in what God in His word promises to do for us *at the very moment of baptism itself.* The work of baptism is truly God's work. In it He has promised to forgive our sins (Acts 2:38; 22:16) and give us the gift of the Holy Spirit (Acts 2:38-39). In it He has

**127**

> **The work of baptism is truly God's work.**

promised to put our old sinful nature to death, to remove it in a kind of spiritual circumcision — a circumcision performed by Christ Himself (Col. 2:11). In it He has promised to raise us up from the dead, to make us alive again, to give us new life (Col. 2:12).

These are truly great and wonderful promises; but if we believe them — if we really believe that God will perform these mighty works upon us in baptism, then we can be assured that He will do it. For those of us who have already been baptized, we can be assured that he has done it. If we can believe that He raised Jesus from the dead, we can be just as sure that He raises us from the dead when we meet Him in the waters of baptism. This is why the last part of verse 12 is there, namely, to remind us that the God who has promised to raise us from the dead in baptism has already demonstrated His willingness and power to do so by raising His own Son from the dead.

This is a great Biblical truth (one that many sadly have completely lost sight of), namely, that baptism at its very heart is "the working of God." The only things we contribute to baptism are *faith* in that promised working, and *prayer* (calling upon His name) for Him to work therein the works of salvation according to His promises. (See again the chapter on Acts 22:16.)

## Baptism and Circumcision

A final point that draws our attention in Colossians 2:11-13 is the relation between baptism and circumcision. For various reasons many Christians believe that baptism is the New Testament replacement for Old Testament circumcision. For some this is an incidental belief, but for others it is the determining factor in their whole doctrine of baptism. It is used not only to prove the validity of infant baptism, but also to define the very meaning of baptism. That is, if baptism simply replaces circumcision, then it must have the same meaning for us today as circumcision had for Old Testament believers. Since circumcision is usually interpreted as a

**128**

sign of membership in the covenant people, this is the meaning assigned to baptism, too. By virtually ignoring everything the New Testament actually says about baptism as God's work of salvation, and by assuming this relationship with circumcision, many Protestants interpret baptism simply as the outward sign that marks one as a member of the church.

It is impossible to overestimate the impact that this equating of circumcision and baptism has had on the doctrine of baptism in modern times.

One of the most striking points in connection with this problem is the fact that outside of Colossians 2:11-13, *no* Biblical passages connect baptism and circumcision *in any* way. With this one exception, the alleged equation of the two is completely inferential. But what about the Colossians passage itself? Isn't one passage enough to establish a doctrinal truth? It would be, if that one passage did indeed teach that truth. And indeed, this is the way Colossians 2:11-13 is often cited, namely, as affirming a continuity in meaning between Old Testament circumcision and New Testament baptism. But does it actually teach this? I believe that it does *not*, and that this can be easily shown as follows.

There are two distinct categories of Old Testament references to circumcision. On the one hand there are many references to physical circumcision as the sign of the covenant God made with Abraham (Gen. 17:10ff) and as the continuing mark of covenant membership under the Law of Moses (Lev. 12:3). On the other hand there are a number of passages which refer to circumcision in figurative senses that have no intrinsic connection to physical circumcision at all. For instance, Moses complains that he is "uncircumcised of lips" (Ex. 6:12,30), meaning that he is an incompetent and unpersuasive speaker. The fruit of certain trees is called "uncircumcised" (Lev. 19:23), meaning forbidden or off-limits like any Gentile.

The most significant figurative sense in this second category is the prophetic use of circumcision and uncircumcision to represent certain spiritual states or conditions of the heart. Jeremiah speaks

**129**

of uncircumcised ears, meaning ears that would not hear the word of God (Jer. 6:10). Others speak of the more basic condition of an uncircumcised heart, meaning a heart filled with sin and rebellious against God, whether Jewish (Lev. 26:41; Jer. 9:26) or Gentile (Ezek. 44:7,9). The Lord exhorted the sinners among Israel to circumcise their hearts: "Circumcise then your heart, and stiffen your neck no more" (Deut. 10:16). "Circumcise yourselves to the Lord and remove the foreskins of your heart" (Jer. 4:4). In what I take to be a Messianic promise God says, "Moreover the Lord your God will circumcise your heart and the heart of your descendants, to love the Lord your God with all your heart and with all your soul, in order that you may live" (Deut. 30:6)

Now, the important point to notice is this: *there is no intrinsic connection between physical circumcision and the state of spiritual circumcision of which the prophets speak.* The former was not given to represent the latter, and the latter was not necessarily present in everyone who had the former. In fact, the relationship between them is casual and incidental. Physical circumcision as the covenant sign was a fact of life within Israel, and as such it served as a convenient and ever-present illustration or analogy for the point the prophets wanted to make about the spiritual state of the heart. Except for this relationship of an incidental analogy, the two kinds of circumcision are independent and unconnected.

How does this relate to baptism and to Paul's teaching in Colossians 2:11-13? In this way: the only Old Testament circumcision to which baptism has *any* relation is the *spiritual* circumcision of which the prophets spoke. Colossians 2:11 speaks of such a circumcision, a change in the inner spiritual condition. In Old Testament times this kind of change was limited to what the individual could bring about for himself; thus the Israelites were exhorted to circumcise their own hearts. But according to the prophecy (Deut. 30:6) there would come a time when God Himself would circumcise the hearts of penitent believers. This I believe refers to the new-age gift of the Holy Spirit, who Himself

> There would come a time when God Himself would circumcise the hearts of penitent believers.

works true regeneration upon the sinner's heart. This is the "circumcision made without hands" of which Colossians 2:11 speaks.

The important point is that *there is no reference to physical circumcision at all in Colossians 2:11-13*. It is present only in the same sense as it was in the prophetic references, namely, as a background analogy. Paul is making no affirmation whatsoever about any relation between baptism and the Abrahamic covenant sign of circumcision. His only reference is to the inner, spiritual circumcision of the heart.[7]

How is this spiritual circumcision related to baptism? Paul says that this marvelous "working of God," this regenerating and life-giving "circumcision of Christ" *takes place in baptism*. It is ironic that a passage which so clearly and forcefully teaches such a strong view of baptism should be used so often in an effort to establish an opposite view.[8] Perhaps it is a matter of uncircumcised ears (Jer. 6:10).

> This regenerating and life-giving "circumcision of Christ" takes place in baptism.

Thus we conclude that the attempt to equate baptism and circumcision based on Colossians 2:11-13 is a misuse of the passage. The alleged equation is without foundation.

## Summary

In this chapter we have seen that Colossians 2:11-13 makes these points. First, baptism is the time when we are buried with Christ into His death to bring about the death of our sinful nature, an event called spiritual circumcision, thus preparing the way for our resurrection to new life. Second, baptism is the time when this resurrection to new life occurs. This resurrection has two senses: we are raised up after we have died *to* sin, and we are raised up out of the state of death *in* sin. Third, though it occurs in baptism, this burial and resurrection with Christ take place *through faith*, thus ruling out baptismal regeneration and infant baptism. Finally, the only circumcision connected with baptism is the spiritual circumcision of the heart, which occurs at the time of baptism. There is no intrinsic relationship between physical circumcision and baptism at all.

## NOTES

1. The complementary nature of these two passages will be discussed in the next chapter when the relationship between baptism and grace is examined.

2. Both here and in verse 11, as in many other places in Paul's epistles, the term *flesh* does not refer to the physical body but to the sinful side of our nature. It has an ethical rather than a metaphysical connotation.

3. This condition may well be called a state of *depravity*, but it should not be confused with the doctrine of *total* depravity. See Jack Cottrell, *His Truth* (Joplin, Mo.: College Press, 1989), 42-46.

4. The NIV, in its usual paraphrastic mode, does not translate *en ho* at all but does retain the sense: "In baptism you were buried with him and raised with him." Both the burial and the resurrection are "in baptism." Some try to make *en ho* refer to Christ ("in whom"), but textual and grammatical considerations rule this out. For a summary of the arguments against this view see Beasley-Murray, *Baptism in the New Testament,* 153-154.

5. See G.W. Bromiley, "Baptismal Regeneration," *Evangelical Dictionary of Theology,* ed. Walter A. Elwell (Grand Rapids: Baker Book House, 1984), 119. On this view baptism is "automatically efficacious," he says.

6. Lutherans have attempted to avoid this conclusion by positing the unique doctrine of infant faith: infants *can* believe, and God implants faith within them when they are baptized.

7. Other New Testament references to this spiritual circumcision include Acts 7:51; Romans 2:25-29; Philippians 3:3. See Ephesians 2:11; Colossians 2:13.

8. The argument runs like this: here in Colossians Paul is equating baptism and Old Testament circumcision; O.T. circumcision was the sign of belonging to the covenant; therefore baptism is the sign of belonging to the covenant — and no more.

# ≈ 12 ≈
# TITUS 3:5

One might expect that, after examining ten New Testament passages about baptism in some detail, we would find little that is new in the last couple of passages. To some extent that is true. Nevertheless it is important to study all of the texts that deal with the meaning of baptism so that we may be impressed with the consistency of the New Testament's teaching on this subject.

This certainly applies to Titus 3:5. There is not much new here in the way of substance, though some of the details of expression are different from what we have thus far encountered. Thus in many ways this chapter will simply confirm the conclusions of the preceding ones, especially on the subject of how baptism relates to the Holy Spirit and regeneration. A subject that has received only scant attention thus far and that will be expanded here is the relation between baptism and grace.

Here is the text we are now considering, along with the full sentence in which it appears (Titus 3:4-7):

> But when the kindness of God our Savior and His love for mankind appeared. He saved us, not on the basis of deeds which we have done in righteousness, but according to His mercy, by the washing of regeneration and renewing by the Holy Spirit, whom He poured out upon us richly through Jesus Christ our Savior, that being justified by His grace we might be made heirs according to the hope of eternal life.

# Baptism and Salvation

The main theme of this passage is salvation. Both the Father (v. 4) and the Son (v. 6) are designated as "our Savior." Verse 4 seems to be referring specifically to the incarnation of Christ and by inference to His general saving work of atonement and resurrection. Verses 5-7, on the other hand, seem to be referring to the application of this salvation to individuals. This is the main point of the passage, namely, how God saves the individual sinner.

The key verb is in verse 5, "He saved us." This is in the aorist tense, which means it is referring to a single past completed action.

> At some specific point in each individual Christian's past there was a single act of God, the effect of which was to save us.

To be sure, there are present and future aspects of salvation that have not been completely worked out yet. Nevertheless at some specific point in each individual Christian's past there was a single act of God, the effect of which was to *save* us. We can say of ourselves that we *have been saved* (Eph. 2:5,8).

The content of this salvation is in essence the "double cure" of forgiveness and regeneration. Verse 7 mentions the former ("being justified") but does not elaborate upon it. The main emphasis falls upon regeneration (also called renewing) in verse 5. Again this refers to the inward change God works upon our hearts when we submit to Him in faith and repentance. It is equivalent to the new birth of John 3:3-5, the dying and rising with Christ of Romans 6:3-5, the spiritual circumcision of Colossians 2:11, and the resurrection and making alive of Colossians 2:12-13.

The two terms for the concept of regeneration used in Titus 3:5 have not been used in any of the passages studied up to this point. The first of these is the Greek word *palingenesia*. Of all the equivalent terms that represent this concept, this is the only one that translates as "regeneration." It is used in the New Testament only here and in Matthew 19:28, where it refers to the eschatological renewing of the entire universe, the "new heavens and new earth." Only here in Titus 3:5 does it refer to the saving regeneration of the individual.

This term is a combination of two Greek words: *palin*, which means "again" ("re-"), and *genesis*, meaning "beginning" or "birth." Thus it means a new beginning, a new birth, a rebirth. Its equivalence to the "born again" of John 3:3 is obvious. In secular Greek literature it is sometimes used in the sense of "coming back from death to life,"[1] which shows its similarity to the resurrection or making alive of Romans 6:3ff and Colossians 2:12-13. Here in Titus 3:5 it includes mainly the idea of "attainment to a new life with the end of the old life," as well as the idea of moral renewal.[2]

The second term, synonymous to the first, is *anakainosis*. It means "renewal," from the verb form meaning "to renew, to make new." It is based on the word *kainos*, which means something new and distinctive as compared with the usual, something new and better as compared with the old.[3] Some think this term differs from regeneration in that the latter refers to an instantaneous event of rebirth while the former refers to an ongoing process of renewal. While it is true that "renewal" sometimes represents such a process (see 2 Cor. 4:16; Col. 3:10), here in Titus 3:5 it is referring to that single past act also called regeneration.

The main point conveyed by both terms is that God *saved* us at that point when He regenerated and renewed us, when He caused us to be born again into a new life that is truly better than the old.

What exactly was that point in time when this salvation occurred? None other than the event called the *washing* (Greek, *loutron*). God saved us, says Paul, by the washing which brings regeneration and renewing. In light of other New Testament uses of the word *loutron* and its verb form, *louo*, it would be unreasonable to deny that this is a reference to baptism. In Oepke's opinion, with three exceptions all the uses of the verb "are related to freeing from sin, and esp. to baptism." The noun *(loutron)* "is used only for this."[4] "All the relevant passages show that, so far as theological usage is concerned," these terms "are baptismal terms."[5] We have already seen how everything related to the washing here in Titus 3:5 (salvation, regeneration, the Holy

**135**

Spirit) is related to baptism in other New Testament passages. "All things considered," says BeasleyMurray correctly, "it requires a real hardiness of spirit to refuse the weight of this evidence."[6]

In this passage baptism is connected to salvation by a very strong term: "He saved us . . . *by* the washing." The Greek word for *by* is *dia*, which with the genitive case (as here) means "by, through, by means of," and can refer to the cause or instrument by which something is brought about or to the time or occasion when it is brought about.[7] This is the same term used in Romans 6:4, which says we were buried with Christ *through* baptism into death (His and ours). Other strong expressions we have already examined are John 3:5, which says we were born again *from (ek)* water; Ephesians 5:26, which says Christ cleansed the church *by* the washing with water (dative of means); and Colossians 2:12, which says we were buried and raised with Christ *in (en)* baptism. *At the very least*, expressions such as these and the one here in Titus 3:5 must be saying that baptism is the *time during which* God has saved us.

The language itself would warrant the stronger *causal* concept, but this is ruled out because (as we have already noted) neither water nor the physical act of baptism can literally cause the dramatic spiritual changes that occur in baptism, and because Scripture specifies that the actual causes of these changes are the blood of Christ and the Holy Spirit (see the next paragraph). But there is *no reason whatsoever* why God could not appoint the act of water baptism as the *time* during which He promises to work these saving changes through these divine causes. And according to the abundant evidence of the New Testament, He has done this.

This passage makes it clear that the true source or cause of our salvation is the full Trinity. In verse 4 "God our Savior" refers to God the Father. That His "kindness . . . and His love for mankind appeared" refers to His sending of God the Son, "Jesus Christ our Savior," who sent God the Holy Spirit (v. 6). The main emphasis of the passage is on the specific work of the Spirit, who is the source of the power that works the regeneration or renewing that takes place in baptism (v. 5),[8] a point already seen in connection with John 3:5, Acts 2:38, and 1 Corinthians 12:13. This should make it clear that we cannot attribute the power of baptism to the water, or to the act itself, or to any-

> We cannot attribute the power of baptism to the water. The power that brings the regeneration and renewing is from the Holy Spirit alone.

thing in the one baptizing or in the one being baptized. The power that brings the regeneration and renewing is from the Holy Spirit alone, who acts in Christian baptism by divine appointment.

Verse 6 says that God "poured out" the Holy Spirit upon us richly through Jesus Christ. The Greek word for "poured out" is *ekcheo* (pronounced ek-KEH-oh), which is also used in Acts 2:17-18 and 2:33 for the initial general outpouring of the Spirit on the day of Pentecost. On that day God promised to give the Spirit to anyone who repents and is baptized in the name of Jesus. That is, He promised an *individual* outpouring that can be enjoyed by anyone who will receive it. Titus 3:5-6 is referring to this out-pouring of the Spirit upon the individual in the moment of baptism. In other words, baptism is the individual's own personal Pentecost.[9]

## Baptism and Grace

We turn now to the very important subject of the relationship between baptism and grace. One of the strongest objections many Protestants have to the understanding of baptism reflected in this book is their earnest conviction that such a view contradicts the Biblical teaching of salvation by grace alone. They rightly stress the grand truth taught in Ephesians 2:8-9, "for by grace you have been saved through faith; and that not of yourselves, it is the gift of God; not as a result of works, that no one should boast." And since they are firmly convinced that baptism as obedience to a command must be in the category of works, they stoutly resist any effort to identify it as the time when God saves us.

We must insist, however, that this supposed contradiction between baptism for salvation and salvation by grace exists only in the minds of men and not in the mind of God. Without any question, the Bible teaches very clearly that we are saved by grace alone. But at the same time, as we have seen, *every single Bible passage* that says anything at all about the meaning of baptism represents it in some way as the time when God bestows His saving grace upon the sinner. This is supremely true of Titus 3:4-7, as we shall now see in more detail.

According to the Bible, there are two separate and different ways in which a person might try to be saved. We may call these the way of *law* and the way of *grace* (see Rom. 6:14). Under the way of law, a person tries to be saved by his own works, viz., by his acts of obedience to the commandments of God in His role as Lord and Lawgiver. Under the way of grace, a person tries to be saved by his faith in the works of God, viz., by his trusting and yielding acceptance of the promises of God in His role as Redeemer and Savior.

Also according to Scripture, the latter way and it alone can save a sinner. It is impossible for a sinner to be saved by the way of law. This is because once a sin has been committed, nothing the sinner can do can ever make up for that sin, even if he could live a perfect life after committing just the one sin — something which in itself becomes a practical impossibility for the sinner. Thus anyone who hopes to be saved must cease trying to be saved by law or works, and must rely on the grace of God alone. This does *not* mean, though, that he should ignore God's law (His commands) and cease to do good works (i.e., to obey the commands). Indeed, works done in obedience to law or commands are an integral part of the Christian life. The law is still normative for our sanctification, though not for our justification and thus our assured salvation.

> It is impossible for a sinner to be saved by the way of law.

Where does baptism fit into all this? The typical Protestant answer is that baptism is part of the law sphere, a work done in obedience to a command. Thus it should be done as a "good work" of the Christian life, as a step in the process of sanctification. But (so it is said) to be baptized in order to be saved is to abandon grace and attempt to be saved by works of law. The fact of the matter, however, is this: the Bible *never* treats baptism as a work of law or as a simple act of obedience in response to a command. Whenever the distinction is relevant to the context, the Bible *always excludes* baptism from the category of law (works, commands) and *includes* it in the category of grace (faith, promises). As we have seen, Matthew 28:18-20 distinguishes baptism from the category of obedience to all of Christ's commands, i.e., from the category of law. In Mark 16:16 and Acts 2:38-39 it is clear that baptism is in essence a promise — another grace concept. In Romans 6:3-4 and Galatians 3:26-27 baptism is presented as a saving act in the very midst of discussions of the law-grace contrast, where the idea that one can be saved by works of law (such as circumcision) is vehemently rejected.

Nowhere is the grace-nature of baptism more evident than here in Titus 3:4-7. The contrast between law and grace as ways of salvation is explicit. We are saved *not* "on the basis of deeds which we have done in righteousness, but according to His mercy, . . . being justified by His grace." The "deeds which we have done in righteousness" are the good works of the Christian life, acceptable to God in themselves but futile for procuring salvation. The only way we can be saved is by His mercy and His grace. Now, the following must be carefully observed. Baptism is clearly distinguished from the category of deeds or works in a pointedly disjunctive contrast: *not* on the basis of deeds *but* by the washing of regeneration and

> **Baptism is clearly distinguished from the category of deeds in a pointed contrast.**

renewing. Also, the reference to the washing is sandwiched comfortably between mercy and grace as a natural and integral part of that whole package. Thus this passage explicitly teaches what is implicit throughout the New Testament, that the baptismal washing is not "works" at all but is truly a matter of grace.

It is not strictly true to say that baptism is not "works" *at all*. More accurately, it is not a *human* work but a *divine* work, a "working of God" — a fact which all the more emphasizes its essence as grace, since the grace-way of salvation is from begin-

**139**

ning to end a matter of *God's* works and not our own. Martin Luther, who better than anyone else has defended the New Testament view of the meaning of baptism, was often accused by his opponents of being inconsistent on this point. How can you teach this view of baptism, they would say, and at the same time teach salvation by grace through faith? Isn't baptism a work, and are not works useless for salvation? Luther's classic reply was this: "Yes, it is true that our works are of no use for salvation. Baptism, however, is not our work but God's," and God's works have saving power and are "necessary for salvation."[10]

If the New Testament teaches anything at all about baptism, it teaches that it is *God's work*. It practically shouts this point, which should be fairly obvious to anyone who has followed the discussion in this book up to now. As we have noted, the only things done by the person being baptized are believing and praying. In everything else the person is completely passive. Even in the physical action he allows someone else to lower him into the water and raise him up out of it. Especially on the spiritual side of baptism he simply calls upon God to work His promised works, and then trusts Him to do it. What are these works? They are union with Christ, especially in His death and resurrection; union with the whole Trinity; the forgiveness or washing away of sins (justification); a clear conscience (see the next chapter); death to sin; the burial of the old nature and resurrection to new life; the gift of the Holy Spirit; regeneration, renewing, the new birth; sanctification; union with the body of Christ; and, in short, salvation. *These* are things the Bible says are worked for us in baptism. They are clearly works of salvation and works which only God Himself can perform, not man.

It is tragic that much of Protestantism has allowed itself to be seduced into thinking and speaking of baptism as almost solely something that man himself does. The following are typical ways of referring to baptism today, not just as descriptions but as expressing its very meaning and essence: in baptism one makes a response, makes a commitment, expresses his faith, testifies to his faith, announces his faith, confirms his salvation, demonstrates his discipleship, or pledges to live the Christian life. What do these actions have in common? For one thing, they are all *human* actions, things *we* do. More significantly, *the Bible never once speaks of baptism in such terms.* Why not? Because in the Bible baptism is thought of not as something *we* are doing but as something *God is* doing. It is indeed "the working of God" (Col. 2:12).

No passage brings out this point better than Titus 3:5. The central thought here is something God has done: "He saved us." In connection with this, two words have an emphatic force, namely, "not" and "we." In the Greek text the word "not" is the very first word in the verse, which means that it is especially to be emphasized. Also in the Greek text the word "we" is usually understood from the form of the verb, but here the pronoun itself is added — something that is done only for emphasis. Thus to discern the proper emphasis, this is how it should be read: "He saved us, *NOT on* the basis of deeds which *WE* have done."

> **Baptism is thus God's work and not man's, and thus a work of purest grace.**

How, then? By baptism! How so? Because this is where God the Holy Spirit works *HIS* work of regeneration and renewing! It could not be made more plain that baptism is thus God's work and not man's, and thus a work of purest grace.

For those who still want to retreat to Ephesians 2:8-10, which seems to summarize the whole picture of salvation without mentioning baptism, we now return to a point mentioned in the last chapter but not developed there. I am speaking of the significance of the parallel between the content of Ephesians 2:1-11 and Colossians 2:11-13. We should remember that these two epistles of Paul are two of his "prison epistles," written at about the same time while he was in prison in Rome. To a large extent they cover the same subjects, though neither letter has all the details contained in the other. Like the Gospels, they supplement one another; they have to be read together for the total picture.

In these two specific passages the subject is the same, namely, how a spiritually dead sinner becomes a living Christian. The chart below shows the identity of the themes and expressions contained therein.

The parallel is obvious and quite striking. Also striking is the fact that the only thing NOT mentioned in Colossians that appears in Ephesians is *grace*, and the only thing NOT mentioned in Ephesians that appears in Colossians is *baptism*! Now, just because grace is not specifically mentioned in Colossians, would anyone dare to suggest that grace does not belong in the way of salvation depicted there? Surely the answer is no. We would all understand, especially in view of the parallel nature of the passages, that grace is simply a detail Paul did not deem necessary to include in Colossians, no doubt because it is so clearly stressed elsewhere. *The same applies to baptism in relation to the Ephesians passage.* Even though it is not specifically mentioned, in view of the parallel we *cannot* deny that it is perfectly consistent with what *is* named there. Combining the thoughts of Ephesians 2:8-10 and Colossians 2:12, we find this Biblical, grace-oriented "plan of salvation": BY GRACE (as the *basis* of salvation); THROUGH FAITH (as *means*); IN BAPTISM (as *time*); FOR GOOD WORKS (as *result*).[11]

|  | Eph. 2 | Col. 2 |
|---|---|---|
|  | (Verses) | (Verses) |
| 1. The sinner's lost state |  |  |
| a) Dead in sins | 1,5 | 13 |
| b) Spiritually uncircumcised | 11 | 13 |
| 2. The Christian's saved state |  |  |
| a) Made alive with Christ | 5 | 13 |
| b) Raised up with Christ | 6 | 12 |
| c) Seated above with Christ | 6 | (3:1-3) |
| d) Spiritually circumcised | 11 | 11,13 |
| 3. How the transition is made |  |  |
| a) By God's work | 10 | 12 |
| b) By grace | 8 |  |
| c) Through faith | 8 | 12 |
| d) In baptism |  | 12 |

If we would allow ourselves truly to hear what the Bible actually says about the meaning of baptism, we would not be able to

Chapter Twelve ◆ TITUS 3:5

resist the following conclusion: nothing is more consistent with salvation by grace than salvation in baptism.

# Summary

In this chapter we have seen first of all how the main subject of Titus 3:4-7 is the salvation of the individual. The content of this salvation is the double cure, with special emphasis being given to regeneration. The time of the regeneration is baptism, and the power that accomplishes it is the Holy Spirit.

The other point covered in this chapter is the relation between baptism and grace. To say that we are saved by (or in) baptism is

> To say that we are saved by (or in) baptism is not a contradiction of grace

not a contradiction of grace, since the Bible never includes baptism in the category of "good works" or obedience to commandments of law. In fact baptism is not a human work at all, but a work of God Himself. Thus we are not surprised that the Bible consistently includes baptism within the sphere of grace.

### NOTES

1. Friedrich Buechsel, γίνομαι, etc.," *Theological Dictionary of the New Testament,* ed. Gerhard Kittel, tr. Geoffrey W. Bromiley (Grand Rapids: Eerdmans, 1964), 1:686.

2. Ibid., 688.

3. Johannes Behm, "καινός, etc.," *Theological Dictionary of the New Testament,* ed. Gerhard Kittel, tr. Geoffrey W. Bromiley (Grand Rapids: Eerdmans, 1965), 111:447.

4. Oepke, "λούω, etc.," 302. The three exceptions refer to secular washing: Acts 9:37; 16:33; 2 Peter 2:22.

5. Ibid., 303.

6. Beasley-Murray, *Baptism in the New Testament,* 210.

7. For a fuller discussion of the term see Albrecht Oepke, "διά," *Theological Dictionary of the New Testament,* ed. Gerhard Kittel, tr. Geoffrey W. Bromiley (Grand Rapids: Eerdmans, 1964), 11:65-70. In Titus 3:5 Oepke says it has the meaning of genitive of *cause* or *instrument:* "by means of, with, through" (66-67).

8. We should note that the syntax or rhythm of the passage is *not* "the WASHING OF REGENERATION (and) the RENEWING OF THE HOLY SPIRIT." but

rather "the WASHING — of the REGENERATION AND RENEWING — of the HOLY SPIRIT."

9. Beasley-Murray says, "The total effect of vv. 5-6 is to represent baptism as the counterpart in the individual's experience of the sending of the Spirit at Pentecost. Baptism is the occasion when the Spirit works creatively in the believer" *(Baptism in the New Testament,* 211).

10. Martin Luther, "The Large Catechism," in *The Book of Concord,* ed. and tr. Theodore G. Tappert (Philadelphia: Fortress Press, 1959), 441.

11. See a more complete explanation of this in my book. *His Truth,* ch. 10, "Truth about Conversion: Man's Response."

# ≈ 13 ≈
# 1 PETER 3:21

The last passage in the New Testament that reflects on the meaning of baptism is 1 Peter 3:21, "And corresponding to that, baptism now saves you — not the removal of dirt from the flesh, but an appeal to God for a good conscience — through the resurrection of Jesus Christ." This is the only statement from Peter's epistles (as compared with six from Paul's), though Acts 2:38 is a quotation from Peter's sermon on Pentecost.

It is quite fitting that this should be the final passage dealt with in this series of studies, since it epitomizes all that has been said thus far. It is especially clear on the central theme of this book, namely, the saving significance of baptism.

## Baptism Saves

Next to Mark 16:16 this is the most straightforward and unequivocal statement in the New Testament concerning the relation between baptism and salvation. In plain words it simply says, "Baptism now saves you." This affirmation is made following some comments on Noah and the ark. Regarding the ark Peter says, "In it only a few people, eight in all, were saved through water" (1 Pet. 3:20, NIV). In some way this water, or this salvation through water, is a type or analogy of the fact that baptism saves people in the New Testament age.

The reference to a type or analogy indicates that there is a figurative connection here somewhere. The King James Version says, "The like figure whereunto even baptism doth also now save us."

Through careless reading some have interpreted this to mean that baptism itself is the figure or symbol that stands for some other reality. Following the prevalent theology of the day, they conclude that baptism thus symbolizes the moment of salvation that has already occurred. But this is just the opposite of what Peter says. The two things being compared are the Noahic flood and baptism, and the relation between them is that of type and antitype. As such the flood is the preceding type or figure, and baptism is the reality to which it points. Thus baptism is not the symbol but the reality itself, and that reality is the fact that *baptism saves.*

Though the nature of the reality is clear enough, exactly how the flood functions as a type of baptism is somewhat difficult to discern. Verse 20 says literally that eight persons were saved through (Greek, *dia*) water. There is some disagreement as to whether "through " *(dia)* means "by means of" (KJV, "by") or "while going through" (NASB, "brought safely through"). In the former case the water is the *instrument* of salvation in the sense that it keeps the ark afloat; in the latter case the water is the *element from which* Noah's family is saved. Some think Peter had both meanings in mind (thus the simple literal translation "through water").[1] He more likely intends the instrumental use, however, since this more readily corresponds to baptism. If we are unaccustomed to thinking of the water of the flood as an instrument of salvation, we are even less prepared to think of the water of baptism as something we must be "brought safely through."

Whatever the precise connection, this fact remains clear: in some sense Noah's family was saved by the water of the flood, and this prefigures the fact that "baptism now saves you." The present tense is used because Peter is referring to "now," in this present age, as compared with "once" or "long ago," in the days of Noah's flood. The water that saved Noah and his family was the water of the flood, but the water that saves us now in our time is the water of baptism.

> Noah's family was saved by the water of the flood, and this prefigures the fact that "baptism now saves you."

# An Appeal to God

Leaving behind the connection with the flood, we now focus on the more important question of *how* baptism saves. The ultimate answer is that it saves through the divine power of the resurrection of Christ, as we will see in the section "Through Christ's Resurrection" below. But before that point is made, Peter comments on how baptism can be said to save us from the standpoint of what we ourselves are doing in the act of baptism. What is there about our own participation in baptism that helps to make it an instrument or channel of salvation?

The answer is given in the form of a contrast: not this, but this. Baptism saves *not* because it is "the removal of dirt from the flesh," *but* because it is "an appeal to God for a good conscience." The negative part of this contrast refers to the outward function of water as a means of washing dirt off the body. (The term *flesh* here refers to the physical body, as in 3:18 and 4:1-2.) Though water is an effective agent for cleansing the body, this is not the way baptism saves. Rather, it saves insofar as it is an appeal to God for a good conscience. This is a reference to the spiritual side of baptism, in contrast with its physical side. The spiritual aspect of baptism is what saves you: not the way it cleanses the body but the way it cleanses the conscience.

We must be careful not to draw the false conclusion that the outward side of baptism or the actual immersion in water is not important, however. Even though it does not save through its physical element of action, it is still *baptism* that saves. This cannot be limited to an alleged spiritual baptism not involving water, since there is only *one baptism* in our Christian experience (Eph. 4:5).[2] Besides this, water is prominent in the context of 1 Peter 3:21. The fact that baptism involves water is what links it with the flood in the first place.

What this text shows is that there is more to baptism than the bare physical action of immersion. Along with that are the spiritual elements and actions

> There is more to baptism than the bare physical action of immersion.

**147**

that accompany it; these too are a part of baptism and are what give it its saving power. One of these saving spiritual elements is the "appeal to God for a good conscience." The key word here is *appeal*, which translates the Greek word *eperotema* (pronounced ep-eh-ROE-tay-mah).

Unfortunately the word *eperotema* is not easy to translate, and it occurs nowhere else in the New Testament so that comparisons might be made with its use in 1 Peter 3:21. Several quite different translations (actually interpretations) have been defended. Some say it should be "the *pledge* of a good conscience," or the pledge to maintain a good conscience before God. This is the translation in the New International Version. Luther used a similar word, *Bund* (meaning covenant or pledge) in his German New Testament. Another suggested meaning is "the *offer* of a good conscience." That is, in baptism God offers to give us a good conscience. This is Lenski's view.[3] Another view is that *eperotema* means *answer* or response, namely, baptism is how a good conscience responds to God. This idea is found in the King James Version. A final view is that the word basically means an *appeal* to God for or by a good conscience (as in the NASB, the RSV, and the NEB). Variations of this are *prayer* (Moffatt's translation) and *request* (Rotherham's Emphasized New Testament).

With so many variations suggested it is difficult to be dogmatic in our translation of the word, but my firm conviction is that the last view is the correct one. The NASB translation is correct; baptism saves as "an appeal to God for a good conscience." The first reason for this choice is the fact that the common meaning for the verb forms of this word is "to ask, to inquire, to request," both inside and outside the New Testament.[4] There is no good reason to deviate from this meaning for the noun form as long as it fits the context of 1 Peter 3:21.

In fact the second reason for adopting this meaning for the word is that it *does* fit the context, especially the connection of baptism with salvation. We must remember that whatever the *eperotema* is, it is an aspect of baptism itself, and especially an aspect of baptism that allows it to be a saving act. Thus the content of the word must be consistent with the fact that salvation is by grace, that it is by God's working and not our own. The meaning we find in *eperotema* must not transform baptism into a work that we perform, but must maintain its character as a saving work of God Himself.

In my opinion this completely rules out the idea of a pledge or vow (as in the NIV). In the first place there is no hint of such an idea associated with baptism anywhere else in the New Testament. But more importantly it is inconsistent with salvation by grace. It would mean that baptism saves us because of its character as a pledge to maintain a good conscience toward God, because in it we are vowing to live a life of obedience to God's commands. But such a pledge is eminently a human act, and more importantly an act that is self-contained or self-climactic. That is, as an action it is complete in itself and does not by its very nature point beyond itself to God's works. This means that a human act or work would become the central element of baptism. And because this passage connects baptism with salvation, this would make the saving essence of baptism reside in something *we* do rather than in something God does. But this would be contrary to grace; thus we reject the view that baptism saves because it is the participant's pledge or vow.

On the other hand, the idea that baptism is the sinner's *answer* or response to God's offer of salvation is consistent with salvation by grace. As such it would be comparable to a beggar holding out an empty hand to receive an offered gift. There is nothing contrary to grace in such a gesture. This view lacks a firm lexicographical basis, though.

The same is true of Lenski's view that the *eperotema* is God's *offer* of a good conscience to be given in baptism. This is eminently consistent with salvation by grace, which is the point Lenski is so concerned to maintain; but this meaning is not warranted by the lexicons. Lenski compensates for this by turning the offer into a question, i.e., "God puts the question before man as to whether he wants to have a good conscience and receives the answer in the believing 'yes' of the one accepting baptism."[5] The problem with this is that this "question" or offer is not given in baptism itself but in the gospel proclaimed before baptism. In this scenario baptism in the end becomes once again the *answer* to the question rather than the question itself.

In the final analysis the meaning both warranted by the lexicons and consistent with the contextual requirements is that of baptism as an appeal or prayer to God for a good conscience. (In this understanding the phrase "to God" or "toward God" [Greek, *eis theon*] goes with "appeal," not "conscience." It is not "a good conscience toward God" but "an appeal to God," as the Greek word order itself suggests.) An appeal is a kind of question, in the sense of a request. Greeven says this meaning may be seen in the verb in Matthew 16:1, and that the noun form in 1 Peter 3:21 may be translated "prayer."[6] Thus baptism is a prayer to God for a good conscience. Even though this prayer is something done by the human participant in baptism, it is consistent with salvation by grace because by its very nature it points beyond itself to God and simply underscores the divine working that is the heart and essence of baptism. The person who submits to baptism is by that very act calling upon God to do what he has promised to do in that moment. Baptism saves because it is the prayer of the human heart crying out to God for spiritual cleansing by His grace. From the standpoint of the human participant this is the most that it *can* be, but that is enough. God himself does the rest.

> Baptism is a prayer to God for a good conscience.

This leads to the third and final reason why *appeal* is the preferred meaning of *eperotema* in 1 Peter 3:21, namely, because this idea is equivalent to the "calling on His name" of Acts 22:16. As we saw in the study of this passage above, in connection with his baptism the sinner Saul was exhorted to call upon the name of the Lord for salvation. That is exactly the point of 1 Peter 3:21. Baptism saves us not because it is something we ourselves are doing but just because it is a prayer that calls upon the name of the only one who has the power to save, our Lord Jesus Christ.

# A Good Conscience

According to the Apostle Peter, in baptism we are praying specifically for "a good conscience." What does this mean? Since it is something we are praying for, it must be a gift given to us by God and received in baptism.[7] In what sense does God *give* us a good conscience?

A person may have a good conscience with respect to both aspects of the double cure of salvation. First, he may have a clear conscience because he does what God commands him to do, because he maintains a holy and pure life before God. God *gives* us a clear conscience in baptism in this sense in that He therein regenerates and renews us through the Holy Spirit, thus making it possible for us to overcome sin and be holy. But this is more the *possibility* of a good conscience than a good conscience itself. Second, a person may have a clear conscience because he has had his sins forgiven, because his guilt and thus his condemnation have been removed (Rom. 8:1) and he is no longer burdened by the pangs of conscience or guilt feelings. God *gives* us a clear conscience in baptism in this sense in that He therein applies the blood of Christ to our guilty souls and gives us forgiveness or remission of sins.

> God gives us a clear conscience in baptism in this sense in that He therein applies the blood of Christ to our guilty souls.

Though both ideas may be included, the main emphasis in 1 Peter 3:21 is probably on the latter. The contrast is between the outward washing of the body, which does not save, and the inward cleansing of the conscience, which does save. Such a complete cleansing is accomplished through the gift of forgiveness by the blood of Christ. This is indicated by a passage which parallels 1 Peter 3:21 in some ways, namely, Hebrews 10:22, "Let us draw near with a sincere heart in full assurance of faith, having our hearts sprinkled clean from an evil conscience and our bodies washed with pure water." This is no doubt a reference to baptism in its outward and inward aspects. The idea that the heart is *sprinkled* from an evil conscience is a reference to the Old Testament practice of sprinkling the blood of sacrificed animals for the purpose of temporary ceremonial cleansing (Heb. 9:13). Its New Testament fulfillment is the spiritual side of baptism, in which the blood of Christ is applied to the heart to cleanse the conscience. As Hebrews 9:14 says, "How much more will the blood of Christ, who through the eternal Spirit offered Himself without blemish to God, cleanse your conscience from dead works to serve the living God?" This is what God promises to do in baptism, and as we enter its waters we claim this promise by appealing to Him to do His work. Thus while the body is being washed with water, He cleanses the heart from its guilt by the blood of Christ; and we emerge from the waters of baptism with a clear conscience.

Greeven sums it up when he says, "Thus the request for a good conscience . . . is to be construed as a prayer for the remission of sins."[8]

## Through Christ's Resurrection

Thus far the question of *how* baptism saves has been answered only in part, and in the lesser part at that. The question has been how baptism as a human act can possibly have a saving force without violating the principle of grace. The answer is that even as a human act it focuses entirely upon the divine action in baptism and shows that the essence of baptism is not anything we do but what God does. The power that saves in baptism is not the power of any human decision or action but the power that comes from God alone.

Now the question can be asked, from what specific divine action comes the saving power of baptism? The answer is, "through the resurrection of Jesus Christ, who is at the right hand of God, having gone into heaven, after angels and authorities and powers had been subjected to Him" (1 Pet. 3:21-22). This is not to slight the power of His blood in any way (see verse 18). It simply acknowledges the fact that in the final analysis everything else, even the atoning death of Christ, depends on His triumphant conquest of death and His eternal reign as the living Lord over all His enemies. Thus even "baptism now saves you . . . through the resurrection of Jesus Christ."

But how exactly does the resurrection of Christ give baptism its saving power? For one thing, it *validates* the extraordinary claims Christ made as well as the work which He had already done. Even the application of His atoning blood in His continuing intercession on our behalf is contingent upon His being brought forth from the dead and being seated at God's right hand. In this sense He "was raised to life for our justification" (Rom. 4:25, NIV). Thus when we appeal to our Lord to give us a good conscience in baptism, we can have confidence that He is alive and that He hears our appeal and that He is able to answer us.

The other way in which Christ's resurrection gives baptism its saving power, and probably the main point, is that it establishes the *authority* of Christ over all things. This is the emphasis in the context, especially verse 22. After the resurrection Jesus was seated at God's right hand, indicating his participation in the full power and authority of the Father. As a result all angels and authorities and powers are in subjection to Him. It was after the resurrection that Jesus laid claim to such full authority: "All authority has been given to Me in heaven and on earth" (Matt. 28:18). The house of Israel may have crucified Jesus; but by raising Him from the dead and exalting Him to His own right hand, "God has made Him both Lord and Christ" (Acts 2:32-36). Being thus exalted, Jesus now has the authority to give gifts to men, i.e., to distribute to us the benefits of His saving work. As Ephesians 4:8 says, "When He ascended on high, He led captive a host of captives, and He gave gifts to men." These gifts would include the gift of forgiveness of sins and thus a good conscience, and the gift of the Holy Spirit. These are what He offers to us in Christian baptism, and this is how baptism saves us through His resurrection.

# Summary

In this chapter we have made four points. First, we have seen that 1 Peter 3:21 states unequivocally that baptism saves. Second, from the standpoint of the human participant, it saves insofar as it is an appeal to God for Him to do what He has promised to do for our salvation. Third, our appeal in baptism specifically is for a good conscience, which comes about through the gift of forgiveness of sins. Finally, the ultimate saving power of baptism is derived from the resurrection of Christ, who as the risen and reigning Lord has the authority to distribute the gifts of salvation as He chooses. And as this passage shows, He chooses to do so in Christian baptism.

> The ultimate saving power of baptism is derived from the resurrection of Christ.

## NOTES

1. Murray J. Harris, "Appendix," 1177.
2. See the discussion of this in chapter 8 on 1 Corinthians 12:13 above.
3. R.C.H. Lenski, *The Interpretation of the Epistles of St. Peter, St. John and St. Jude* (Minneapolis: Augsburg, 1966), 170-173.
4. Heinrich Greeven, "ἐρωτάω, etc.," *Theological Dictionary of the New Testament*, ed. Gerhard Kittel, tr. Geoffrey W. Bromiley (Grand Rapids: Eerdmans, 1964), II: 685-687; G.T.D. Angel, "Prayer [section on ἐρωτάω]," *The New International Dictionary of New Testament Theology*, ed. Colin Brown (Grand Rapids: Zondervan. 1976), 11:879-880.
5. Lenski, *Interpretation of the Epistles of St. Peter,* 172. He is quoting Schlatter but gives no bibliographical data.
6. Greeven, "ἐρωτάω), etc.," 688.
7. Thus the "good conscience" in this verse is not something we are *pledging* to maintain, nor is it what is *motivating* us to be baptized.
8. Greeven, "ἐρωτάω, etc.," 688.

# CONCLUSION

**W**e recognize that the view of the meaning of baptism presented here is very different from the view held by most Protestants, but we earnestly contend that it is the New Testament's own view and that the content of the texts themselves cannot be construed in any other way. Altogether we have studied twelve separate texts in detail, with references to several others along the way. What is remarkable is not only the fact that they *do* present baptism as the time God has appointed for initially bestowing salvation upon believing, repentant sinners, but also the fact that they are *unanimous* in doing so. This is not some obscure inference that must be laboriously forced from the fringes of a few texts, but is the central theme of them all! And at the same time, no other meaning emerges to serve in even a secondary role, much less to challenge the one main idea that baptism is for salvation.

I believe that no one can study these texts objectively and then deny that this is the meaning of baptism, without developing a troubled conscience. And just as baptism itself is an appeal to God for a good conscience, I present this book as an appeal to my friends and brethren to have a clear conscience about baptism. It can be done, if we are willing to listen to the voice of Scripture and to judge our traditions by its clear and pure words alone.

> I believe that no one can study these texts objectively and then deny that this is the meaning of baptism.

But many will surely respond that the other view of baptism — that it is the "sign and seal" of salvation previously received — has

**155**

prevailed for so long that there surely *must* be some validity to it. And even if we decide that it is not valid, how can we change it without upsetting centuries of tradition and ecclesiastical structures and doctrinal systems?

In relation to these serious concerns I will make just two remarks at this time. First, the "other" view of baptism, the one that prevails in most of Protestantism now, is really not very old in comparison with the one presented here as the Biblical view. The understanding of baptism as the time when God bestows salvation was the nearly unanimous view in Christendom for nearly fifteen hundred years. It was a consensus shared by the early church fathers, Catholic theology in the Middle Ages, and Martin Luther. The "other" view, the one that now prevails, was the creation of Huldreich Zwingli in the decade of the 1520s.[1] It was adopted by his followers, including John Calvin; and mainly through the latter's influence was spread throughout the bulk of Protestantism. Thus the "sign and seal" concept of baptism is the newcomer, the usurper. We should have no qualms about abandoning a view whose roots go back no further than Zwingli. We should rejoice in the prospect of embracing a view that is rooted in the New Testament itself and which enjoyed a millennium and a half of unshaken dominance until the usurper arose.

The second comment is addressed to those who fear that such a drastic change in our understanding of baptism would constitute a dreadful judgment of some kind on the past few centuries and especially on the countless sincere believers who have accepted the Zwinglian view and kind of baptism. My comment is a quotation from Cyprian, who in the third century A.D. dealt extensively with the problem of "heretic baptism," viz., whether baptism received in heretical sects was true baptism or not. Cyprian declared that it was not, and that anyone leaving such a sect and coming into an orthodox church should receive true baptism for his salvation. But this practice had not consistently been followed, and some were concerned about what this would imply regarding former heretics who had been accepted into the church without any further baptism. Thus they were reluctant to accept Cyprian's view, even though they might grant it was true, because it required such a negative judgment about past practices and possibly even about the spiritual status of those who had not conformed to this truth previously. Here is Cyprian's wise comment, one which I believe applies in the similar situation of today:

> But some one says, "What, then, shall become of those who in past times, coming from heresy to the Church, were received without baptism?" The Lord is able by His mercy to give indulgence, and not to separate from the gifts of His Church those who by simplicity were admitted into the Church, and in the Church have fallen asleep. Nevertheless it does not follow that, because there was error at one time, there must always be error; since it is more fitting for wise and God-fearing men, gladly and without delay to obey the truth when laid open and perceived, than pertinaciously and obstinately to struggle against brethren and fellow-priests on behalf of heretics.[2]

## NOTES

1. See my unpublished doctoral dissertation, "Covenant and Baptism in the Theology of Huldreich Zwingli" (Princeton, NJ: Princeton Theological Seminary, 1971). My work on Zwingli and baptism is summarized in chapter 2 of the book edited by David Fletcher, *Baptism and the Remission of Sin: An Historical Perspective* (Joplin, MO: College Press, 1990), 39-81.

2. Cyprian, Epistle 72:23, "The Epistles of Cyprian," tr. Ernest Wallis, *The Ante-Nicene Fathers*, ed. Alexander Roberts and James Donaldson (New York: Scribner's, 1886; reprint. Grand Rapids: Eerdmans, 1978), V:385. (The use of this quotation does not imply that those who follow the Zwinglian view of baptism should be labeled *heretics*.)

# BIBLIOGRAPHY

Angel, G.T.D. "Prayer [section on ἐρωτάω]," *The New International Dictionary of New Testament Theology,* ed. Colin Brown. Grand Rapids: Zondervan, 1976. 11:879-881.

Arndt, William F., and F. Wilbur Gingrich. *A Greek-English Lexicon of the New Testament and Other Early Christian Literature.* 4 ed. Chicago: University of Chicago Press, 1952.

Beasley-Murray, G.R. *Baptism in the New Testament.* Grand Rapids: Eerdmans, 1962.

Behm, Johannes. "καινός, etc." *Theological Dictionary of the New Testament,* ed. Gerhard Kittel, tr. Geoffrey W. Bromiley. Grand Rapids: Ecrdmans, 1965. 111:447-454.

Bietenhard, Hans. "ὄνομα, etc." *Theological Dictionary of the New Testament,* ed. Gerhard Friedrich, tr. Geoffrey W. Bromiley. Grand Rapids: Eerdmans, 1967. V:242-283.

Bromiley, G.W. "Baptismal Regeneration." *Evangelical Dictionary of Theology,* ed. Walter A. Elwell. Grand Rapids: Baker Book House, 1984.

Buechsel, Friedrich. "γίνομαι, etc." *Theological Dictionary of the New Testament,* ed. Gerhard Kittel, tr. Geoffrey W. Bromiley. Grand Rapids: Eerdmans, 1964. 1:681-689.

Cottrell, Jack. "Are Miraculous Gifts the Blessing of Pentecost?" *Christian Standard* (May 9, 1982), 117:9-11.

_____. "Covenant and Baptism in the Theology of Huldreich Zwingli." Princeton, NJ: Princeton Theological Seminary, 1971, unpublished doctoral dissertation.

_____. *His Truth*. Joplin, Mo.: College Press, 1989 reprint.

_____. *Thirteen Lessons on Grace: Being Good Enough Isn't Good Enough*. Joplin, Mo.: College Press, 1988 reprint.

_____. *What the Bible Says About God the Redeemer*. Joplin, Mo.: College Press, 1987.

_____. *What the Bible Says About God the Ruler*. Joplin, Mo.: College Press, 1984.

Cyprian. "The Epistles of Cyprian," tr. Ernest Wallis. *The Ante-Nicene Fathers*, ed. Alexander Roberts and James Donaldson. New York: Scribner's, 1886; reprint Grand Rapids: Eerdmans, 1978. V.-275-409.

Greeven, Heinrich. "ἐρωτάω, etc." *Theological Dictionary of the New Testament*, ed. Gerhard Kittel, tr. Geoffrey W. Bromiley. Grand Rapids: Eerdmans, 1964. 11:685-689.

Harris, Murray J. "Appendix: Prepositions and Theology in the Greek New Testament." *The New International Dictionary of New Testament Theology*, ed. Colin Brown. Grand Rapids: Zondervan, 1978. 111:1171-1215.

Lenski, R.C.H. *The Interpretation of the Epistles of St. Peter, St. John and St. Jude*. Minneapolis: Augsburg, 1966.

Luther, Martin. "The Large Catechism." *The Book of Concord*, ed. and tr. Theodore G. Tappert. Philadelphia: Fortress Press, 1959. 357-461.

McGarvey, J.W. *Lands of the Bible*. Philadelphia: Lippincott, 1881.

Nash, Donald. "Water and Baptism." *Christian Standard* (April 30, 1978), 113:396-398.

Oepke, Albrecht. "βάπτω, etc." *Theological Dictionary of the New Testament*, ed. Gerhard Kittel, tr. Geoffrey W. Bromiley. Grand Rapids: Eerdmans, 1964. 1:529-546.

_____. "διά." *Theological Dictionary of the New Testament*, ed. Gerhard Kittel, tr. Geoffrey W. Bromiley. Grand Rapids: Eerdmans, 1964. 11:65-70.

_____. "λούω, etc." *Theological Dictionary of the New*

*Testament,* ed. Gerhard Kittel, tr. Geoffrey W. Bromiley. Grand Rapids: Eerdmans, 1967. **IV:** 295-307.

Seymour, Richard A. *All About Repentance.* Hollywood, FL: Harvest House, 1974.

Von Soden, Hans. "ἀδελφός, etc." *Theological Dictionary of the New Testament,* ed. Gerhard Kittel, tr. Geoffrey W. Bromiley. Grand Rapids: Eerdmans, 1964. 1:144-146.

# STUDY GUIDE

## Chapter 1: Matthew 28:19-20

1. In the Great Commission, why is it important that baptism is distinguished from the "all things" that disciples are to be taught? (p. 12)

2. In 1 Corinthians 1:10-17, why did Paul state that he was glad that he only baptized a few of the Corinthians? How does this passage emphasize the importance of baptism? (pp. 13-15)

3. Is baptism simply a good work following Christian salvation? Why or why not? (pp. 12-16)

4. Discuss the significance of being baptized "into the name" of the Father, Son, and Holy Spirit. (pp. 16-17)

5. How is the content of our faith fuller and more complete under the New Covenant than it was under the Old Covenant? (pp. 18-20)

6. Why is it a "serious error" to equate the baptism practiced by John the Baptist with Christian Baptism? (pp. 20-22)

## Chapter 2: Mark 16:15-16

1. The text of Mark 16:9-20 may not have been a part of the original Gospel of Mark. Does this affect our understanding of the biblical doctrine of baptism? Why or why not? (pp. 23-24)

2. How are faith and baptism understood to be similar in Mark 16:16? (pp. 24-25)

3. In Mark 16:16, how is baptism related to salvation? (pp. 25-26)

4. Salvation is linked to baptism by the phrase "he who believes and has been baptized shall be saved." However, baptism is omitted in the next phrase, "he who has disbelieved shall be condemned." Why? (pp. 26-27)

5. Dr. Cottrell points out that when an individual is baptized, he is not so much "obeying a command" as "accepting a promise." Why is this an important understanding about baptism? (pp. 29-31)

## Chapter 3: John 3:3-5

1. In John 3:5, some have viewed the "water" in Jesus' teaching to refer to something other than Christian baptism. What are the two major alternatives? Why are they not the best understanding of the verse? (pp. 34-35)

2. Why would it have been natural for Nicodemus to understand Jesus' reference to "water" in John 3:5 as referring to "water baptism"? (pp. 35-37)

3. Discuss what Jesus meant when he spoke of "the kingdom of God" in John 3:5. (pp. 37-39)

4. Today, there is much discussion and use of the phrase "born again." What does it mean to be "born again"? (pp. 39-40)

5. How does Jesus' teaching in John 3:3-5 help us understand the relationship between baptism and salvation? (pp. 40-43)

# Chapter 4: Acts 2:38-39 (1)

1. Why is the teaching on baptism in Acts 2:38-39 so crucial? (pp. 45-46)

2. What is the "double cure" from sin, which is promised in the gospel? (pp. 48-49)

3. How is repentance related to faith in Peter's response to the crowd at Pentecost? (pp. 50-51)

4. Why do some people seem to have difficulty accepting baptism as a condition of forgiveness and receiving the gift of the Spirit? (p. 51)

5. Why is it essential to understand baptism in Acts 2:38-39 as a reference to "water baptism"? (pp. 51-52)

# Chapter 5: Acts 2:38-39 (2)

1. Discuss the Old Testament imagery of water being associated with the forgiveness of sins. How is Christian baptism a more specific and clear representation of this forgiveness? (pp. 55-57)

2. In Acts 2:38-39, in the phrase "for the forgiveness of sins," the word translated "for" is the Greek word "*eis.*" Discuss the three possible meanings of this Greek word in relationship to forgiveness of sins. Does Dr. Cottrell's interpretation seem to be correct? Why? (pp. 58-60)

3. Discuss the comfort afforded to Christians by the knowledge that, at baptism, we are forgiven of all sins (past, present, and future). (p. 61)

4. Discuss the times in Acts (2:1-4; 10:44-48) when the Holy Spirit was given before baptism. Why should these be seen as "special cases" and not the norm for all Christians? (pp. 62-64)

5. Why is Acts 2:38-39 an excellent summary of receiving Christ by faith? (pp. 64-65)

# Chapter 6: Acts 22:16

1. When Ananias addressed Saul in Acts 22:16, was Saul already saved or was he still an unsaved sinner? Why is it important to answer this question? (pp. 68-71)

2. Dr. Cottrell lists four reasons why baptism is a preceding condition for the forgiveness of sins. Discuss his arguments. (pp. 72-73)

3. Several New Testament passages discuss the concept of "washing" (1 Cor 6:11; Heb 10:22; Eph 5:26; Titus 3:5). How does this passage in Acts 22:16 clarify those other passages? (pp. 73-74)

4. Saul was instructed to "call upon the name of the Lord." Discuss how this relates to baptism. How would this have applied to Saul in the context of the Acts 22 passage? How does it apply to us today? (pp. 74-76)

5. What does Acts 22:16 say to Christians today about the importance of baptism? (p. 76)

# Chapter 7: Romans 6:3-4

1. In Romans 6:3-4, what does the phrase "baptized *into* Christ Jesus" mean? Discuss the significance of what this means to us in our daily lives. (pp. 80-81)

2. Christians have disagreed as to exactly when our "death to sin" occurs. Dr. Cottrell lays out three main positions. Discuss their strengths and shortcomings. Do you agree with Dr. Cottrell's conclusions? (pp. 82-85)

3. How does the teaching on baptism in Romans 6:3-4 point to immersion as the only valid form of baptism? (pp. 85-86)

4. In thinking about the "double cure" for sin, what aspect of the "double cure" relates to our "dying to sin"? (p. 87)

5. Why should a correct understanding of baptism give the Christian a strong motivation for holy living? (pp. 87-88)

# Chapter 8: 1 Corinthians 12:13

1. Discuss the differences between the Reformed, Wesleyan, and traditional Restoration Movement views of what it means to be "baptized in the Spirit." (pp. 93-94)

2. What is Dr. Cottrell's alternative view? How is it different from the three views mentioned above? Do you agree with his reasoning? Why? (pp. 94-95)

3. Discuss the relationship between water and Spirit in the "one baptism" of Ephesians 4:5. (pp. 95-96)

4. What is the difference between what Dr. Cottrell calls the "visible church" and the "invisible church"? Does it appear to you that such a distinction is biblically valid? (pp. 97-98)

5. Why is it important to understand that the reference to the church in 1 Corinthians 12:13 is to the "invisible church"? (pp. 99-100)

6. How does 1 Corinthians 12:13 speak to the unity of all Christians? What is the basis of this unity? (pp. 100-101)

# Chapter 9: Galatians 3:26-27

1. How do the "blessings of Abraham," mentioned in Galatians 3:14, relate to Christians? (p. 104)

2. Galatians 3:16 tells us that Jesus is the one true heir to the promises God made to Abraham. How does this relate to Christians who are "in Christ"? (pp. 104-105)

3. Discuss the different aspects of the biblical image of being "clothed with Christ." How is this an encouragement to us in our Christian life? (pp. 105-107)

4. How do both faith and baptism relate in our becoming "sons of God" through union with Christ? (pp. 107-108)

5. How do the concepts of circumcision and baptism differ in the context of Galatians 3? (pp. 111-112)

# Chapter 10: Ephesians 5:25-27

1. What does it mean for the Christian to be "sanctified"? Discuss the two different aspects of sanctification, noting their unique features. (pp. 116-119)

2. How does the concept of a "cleansed" church relate to the doctrine of justification? Why must Christ "cleanse" the church before He can "sanctify" the church? (pp. 120-121)

3. What argument does Dr. Cottrell put forth to identify the phrase "washing with water" with Christian baptism? Do you find this argument sound? (pp. 121-122)

4. How does the cleansing we receive in baptism bring us into contact with the blood of Christ? (pp. 122-123)

5. What part does the "Word of God" play in uniting the blood of Christ and water baptism? (pp. 123-124)

6. In view of what Christ has done for us, how should our baptism inspire us toward holy (sanctified) living? (pp. 124-125)

# Chapter 11: Colossians 2:11-13

1. What reasons does Dr. Cottrell give for his claim that Colossians 2:11-13 is perhaps the most important passage in the New Testament on the meaning of Christian baptism? (pp. 127-128)

2. Discuss the relationship of the similar themes in Romans 6:1-11 and Colossians 2:11-13 (i.e., burial with Christ; death to sin; dying to sin). (pp. 128-130)

3. Colossians 2:11-13 seems to indicate that the time of our burial with Christ, as well as our being raised with Christ, occurs at Christian baptism. Does this negate the importance of faith? Why not? (pp. 128-135)

4. What problems arise in equating baptism as simply the New Covenant replacement for the Old Covenant rite of circumcision? (pp. 135-137)

5. What is the connection between baptism and circumcision in the context of Colossians 2:11-13? (pp. 137-139)

# Chapter 12: Titus 3:5

1. Dr. Cottrell has discussed the "double cure" of salvation in almost every chapter. How does this relate to the passage in Titus 3:4-7? (pp. 142-143)

2. What two terms for "regeneration" does Paul use in this passage? How are they similar in definition? (pp. 143-144)

3. Discuss the meaning of the phrase, "He saved us . . . by the washing." What does this teach us about the importance of baptism? Do you agree with Dr. Cottrell's statement that "baptism is the individual's own personal Pentecost"? (pp. 144-146)

4. Christians are saved by God's grace (Eph. 2:8-9). How can baptism also be a part of God's saving plan without contradicting the sufficiency of God's grace? (pp. 146-149)

5. Paul separates baptism from "deeds which we have done in righteousness." If baptism is not a human work, what is it? (pp. 148-150)

# Chapter 13: 1 Peter 3:21

1. Discuss the analogy between Noah's family being "saved through water," and baptism's part in "saving" the Christian. (pp. 154-155)

2. The NIV translation states that baptism is the "pledge of a good conscience to God." Why is this not the best translation? What should the translation be? Why? (pp. 156-159)

3. In what sense does God give a "good conscience" when we are baptized? (pp. 159-161)

4. Discuss how the resurrection of Christ gives baptism its saving significance. (pp. 161-162)

5. Dr. Cottrell summarized four main points made in this chapter. Identify them. Do you agree with each one? Why or why not? (pp. 162-163)

# Conclusion

1. Why would the conclusions drawn from this biblical study of baptism "disturb" many people in the evangelical world? (pp. 165-166)

2. Dr. Cottrell makes two final observations about this study. Identify and discuss each one. (pp. 166-167)

3. Has your study of God's word in regard to baptism caused you to change your thinking about this vital topic? If so, in what manner?

4. Discuss how a biblical understanding of baptism can give encouragement to Christians for daily living.